MAGGIE THE MAGNIFICENT

This edition published 2017
By Living Book Press
147 Durren Rd, Jilliby, 2259
Copyright © The Estate of C.K. Thompson, 1950

The publisher would like to give a huge 'Thank You' to the author's family
for their assistance in making this book available once more.

National Library of Australia Cataloguing-in-Publication entry:

Creator:	Thompson, C.K. (Charles Kenneth), 1904-1980
Title:	Maggie the magnificent / C.K. Thompson ; introduction by A.H. Chisholm.
ISBN:	9780648035695 (paperback)
Target Audience:	For primage school age.
Subjects:	Australian magpie--Juvenile fiction.
	Nature stories, Australian.
	Australia--Juvenile fiction.
Other Creators/ Contributors:	Chisholm, Alec H. (Alec Hugh), 1890-1977, writer of introduction.

MAGGIE THE MAGNIFICENT

By C.K. Thompson

(author of "King of the Ranges," "Monarch of the Western Skies," "Warrigal the Warrior," etc)

With Introduction by A. H. Chisholm, F.R.Z.S., (Former President of the Royal Australian Ornithologists' Union, Former President of the field Naturalists' Club of Victoria, Advisor to the Queensland Government on Fauna Protection, etc.)

20 LIVING BOOK PRESS 17

DEDICATION

This story of one of Australia's most popular native birds is dedicated, with sympathy and with fellow feeling, to all my readers, young and old, who have been attacked and pecked by magpies.

Many years ago, when my brother Osmond and I were small boys, we set out, as too many youngsters have done and will do, to rob a magpie's nest. We thought that a young bird would make an excellent pet. We saw the nest, but the parent bird saw us first. On the back of my head I still bear a faint scar where the beak of that indignant bird penetrated.

In later years I have been attacked by magpies on the golf links and I have had golf balls stolen by these black and white villains. In many ways I have cause to say nasty things about them, but I don't. I regard the magpie as the finest of our useful Australian feathered songsters.

Those of us who have suffered at the beaks of magpies may feel that we have a perfect right to be indignant. But have we ever troubled to ascertain Maggie's point of view?

I think that every Australian admires bravery and daring and certainly Maggie possesses those qualities. Thief and villain he might be, but we cannot gainsay his numerous good qualities.

Maggie is entitled, as every Australian is, to "a fair go." In this book I have tried to give it to him.

—C. K. THOMPSON.

MAGGIE

A TRIBUTE

Maggie's just a piping crow
Other birds might tell us;
But, if you would like to know
I believe they're jealous.
Maggie's notes so rich and clear,
With his mate's song blending
Ring afar when dawn is here,
To the bushland's ending.
Like two cheery cooper's men
Rolling out the barrels,
Maggie's male joins with him when
Maggie magpie carols.

Maggie is a pretty sight—
Bold and dark and splendid
In his dress of black and white
All so neatly blended.
Maggie's mate is good to see,
Though I fear that often
Her young heart's queer coquetry
Is too tough to soften
Till her male aloft ascends,
In the gum-tops fading,
And from there his songs descend
In his serenading.'

Loud and liquid, round and true,
flute-like, then a yodel
Its rich music running through.
Maggie's mate's a model—
Knows just what a song should be;
From one heart appealing
To another, which is free
Yet without much feeling
Till the magic in his song
Pierces through her armour
And she yields and sings along
With her black-eyed charmer.

Maggie's mate's a thief; like her
Golf balls, how she'll chase them!
Bits of glass or silverware
In their nest they place them
To be ornaments that make
Home a place of beauty—
Somewhere where a bird may take
Friends in love or duty;
Then the thieves and all these friends
Sing loud songs of gloating;
To the bushland's utter ends
Marking songs go floating.

Humans who through Maggie's guile
With him to perdition,
Pause to listen with I smile
To this bold musician.
He's no foe, but useful friend:
All the farmers praise him;
To his tree their thanks ascend,
Wouldn't that amaze him!
Bold protector of the nest
In his pied regalia;
Maggie typifies the best—
Spirit of Australia.'

—WILL LAWSON.

INTRODUCTION

WHEN I was a boy in the bush of Victoria, I became closely acquainted with the handsome black-and-white birds which we know as Magpies. The acquaintance was, in fact, too close to be pleasant, for one old warrior in particular, whenever the nesting season came round, used to make a practice of swooping from a gum-tree and striking me heartily on the head.

That bird's tactics were very annoying. It was not his blows, but the unequal way in which he distributed them, that mattered most. He did not attack any men in the area. Nor did he ever assail a girl. All his aggression was expended on me—the only boy living in the area.

Why this "favouritism"? Why did the bird neglect men and concentrate his attacks on a boy? Asking myself these questions, I could find only one explanation, and that was that Maggie had learned from hard experience that boys are, or were, apt to be a menace to the welfare of nesting birds. As it chanced, I had never robbed a magpie's nest, but apparently some other lads had offended that particular bird and so, after all, it seemed that the attacks were more or less justified. At the least, they revealed the bird to be possessed of two notable qualities, namely, intelligence and pluck.

In later years I learned to esteem magpies for other reasons. I do so still. They are, of course, very useful as insect-eaters. In addition, their individual or company carols, uttered at dawn or dusk, or even on moonlight nights, exercise a strong appeal. And, for another thing, their sturdy bodies and strong flight make them distinctive figures—the most commanding of all the black-and-white birds which are such a striking feature of the open spaces of this country.

In short, magpies express in no small measure the true Spirit of Australia. Shrewdness, courage, melody, poise and usefulness—what more could you expect any bird to possess? In those qualities lie the reason why it was once suggested that the name "magpie" should be changed to "Anzac-bird."

It follows that Mr. C. K. Thompson's tribute to the magpie, as contained in this book, is well merited. I hope that the story will lead many people to regard the bird even more kindly than they do now. I hope, too, that it will cause popular interest in birds generally to deepen.

Australia's birds, as a whole, are a highly attractive band. Ranging from the giant emu to the tiny emu-wren, they include some of the most beautiful and some of the most interesting groups to be found anywhere. Because of that, and because nearly all of them are of high value—for without them we would probably not have any gardens or crops—there is a duty resting on Australians to ensure that they are safeguarded.

While common-sense demands that birds be protected, patriotism suggests that they should be studied by more people. You cannot very well say with pride, "This is my own, my native land," unless you really know something about your land; and you can best acquire such knowledge by beginning with the prettiest and most useful of all our products—the native birds.

-ALEC H. CHISHOLM.

Contents

Chapter I.

OLD BROKEN BEAK

IT WAS one of those delightful mornings of late winter after the Frost King had made his last defiant gesture. True, the early morning air still had the power to chill, but as the grey turned to primrose and the primrose to red, heralding glorious bars of light that sprang up across the eastern sky, so did the wintry air become warmer.

Soon the golden gates flew open and the sun himself came forth majestically with a radiation of a million flashing spears, their golden tips urging a sleeping world into wakefulness.

The first rays of the rising sun, striking through the leaves of a huge ironbark—an ancient forest giant that had graced this grazing paddock for many years—caressed a fluffy feathered ball of black and white, and then passed on to another, and yet another, playing over them in gentle reproof that these sleepy birds should waste one single moment of what promised to be a perfect day.

Then, out from another great old gum tree on the other side of the paddock, came the first tribute to the God of Light—a haunting, liquid, flute-like melody in a glorious rush of choral splendour. It was fitting that the sun's majesty should be accorded first homage by the loveliest voice in the Australian bush, the magpie's.

There were several trees in this paddock and each was

I

used during the autumn and winter nights as a roosting place by a colony of magpies. The first bird to awaken was the bugler for the regiment and others answered his magic notes with chords of equal beauty before commencing the serious business of the day.

These bold black and white birds were jealous of their territory. A flock of from ten to fifteen worked this particular paddock. All over Australia, similar flocks of magpies would be working similar paddocks, parks, bushlands and farms, and would continue to work them until early spring. In the mating season, which commenced about August, they would pair off and depart to find nesting territory of their own. Some weeks would elapse yet before this occurred and in the meantime the daily routine, observed throughout late summer, the autumn and winter, had to be carried out.

As day succeeded day, so would the rays of the sun get stronger. Already the grass was taking on a greener hue and the wild things realised instinctively that spring was on the way.

The sun was still busily awaking other creatures in the paddock when the first magpies dropped from their over-night roosts energetically to search for their breakfasts. It was every bird for itself, too. Sharp eyes behind sharp beaks caught the slightest movement in the grass that betrayed the presence of an unwary grasshopper, beetle or caterpillar.

Unlike some other birds, the magpies did not wander far and wide in search of food. They had their recognised hunting ground and they stayed in it, ready to defend it against interlopers. They did not invade the chosen haunts of other birds and, therefore, they expected strangers to keep away from theirs.

Grasshoppers were their favorite morsels and these, fortunately for the birds if not for the farmers, were always plentiful. All kinds of crawly things were acceptable and they used their very efficient beaks as spades to dig if required, or as crowbars to turn over stones and manure to get at the creatures beneath. Unwary mice coming out of their burrows to observe the upper world, or lizards caught off guard, were readily seized upon by the sharp-eyed magpies and, after being beaten on a stone, made a most acceptable addition to the breakfast table.

Sometimes the birds temporarily would leave their exclusive paddock for brief visits to nearby cultivated fields in the wheat-growing season and lunch off newly-germinated grain, much to the annoyance of the farmer who had planted it; some of them had been known, too, to emulate their cousins, the butcher birds, and swoop upon some unfortunate lark, sparrow or robin, as an addition to the larder.

Though the flock of magpies lived together sociably, there was no recognised leader. Each individual bird insisted on his or her own rights and did not look to any other for help or guidance.

But there was one old magpie more pugnacious than the rest. He was a battle-scarred veteran with part of the top beak broken and his neck almost bare of feathers which made him look like a miniature vulture. The broken beak, which did not inconvenience him at all, had been caused many years before by a bullet fired from a rifle by a man who had become tired of being attacked as he crossed a field in which the old magpie's nest stood in a big ironbark tree.

Year in and year out, old Broken Beak and a mate had nested in that tree and nothing short of death or dire disaster would prevent him continuing to nest there for the rest of his life. That was his magpie way. Tradition and habit were deeply ingrained.

Old Broken Beak, in his time, had seen many magpies come and go, including several of his own mates. Though most of the present members of the flock had worked that same hunting ground for years, Broken Beak was the oldest, the patriarch of them all. When he first saw the light of day, he had had a brother and two sisters in the nest and they had all taken up residence in this paddock with their parents as soon as they were old enough to look after themselves. His two sisters, in due course, had found mates of their own and had departed for fresh pastures. His brother had found a mate also, and though, in nesting time, they departed to a secluded place in the distant bush, they always returned to the paddock in between keeping house.

This had been the routine for several seasons and then one year his brother's mate had returned alone. What had happened to his brother, Broken Beak did not know. Neither did he care, for Broken Beak had regarded him as just one more magpie. There were no family bonds between them as would be the case among humans.

Though magpies came and went as the years rolled by, there were always about a dozen of them working this huge paddock, Broken Beak among them. He had lost several mates, victims to rifles, the catapults of small boys, accidents and natural deaths. Others had deserted him for more handsome and more amiable husbands.

But this did not cause him the least concern. He was a self-centred bird, independent and more than a little conceited. Up to the present he had never had much trouble finding a mate when the pairing season came round.

He had been the part-architect of many nests. In his time he had built them in trees, among telephone wires and even attempted, on one occasion, to erect one in a house chimney. He had lost nests through human agency; he had been burned out by bushfires and washed out by torrential rain; and he had fought off marauders of all kinds, from small boys to goannas and tiger cats.

Broken Beak was not a popular bird with members of the flock. He just could not mind his own business. He was continually interfering in the affairs of other magpies, specially those who unearthed particularly attractive morsels during their foraging. He had been known to spring upon a bird and try to wrest from him a big centipede that the finder had picked up from under a stone he had overturned with his most-efficient beak, and to chase another and fight him for a mouse he had caught.

Naturally, he did not get his own way on any occasion. Fiercely jealous of their own rights, acknowledging no superior, and afraid of nothing, each magpie was prepared to fight any other bird in defence of those rights. In all his contests with the others, Broken Beak had never once encountered a bird that had turned tail and refused to fight him. Indeed, it would have astonished him if he had ever met a cowardly magpie.

As the days ran on, there were growing signs of restlessness among the flock, and presently pairs of birds began to leave. The mating season was upon them and they had to obey Mother Nature's strongest and most insistent call. And when the flock had dwindled away almost to nothing, old Broken Beak alone had not found a new mate. It did not worry him. He was profoundly confident of his own powers of attraction, though he might have changed his opinion if he could have seen himself in a mirror.

At last there came the day when he was left entirely on his own. His favorite nesting place, the paddock with the ironbark tree, was several miles away, and though he did not yet have a mate to share it, he deemed it wise to go there and enter into possession, just in case some feathered squatter decided to take over in his absence.

It was a first class nesting place, that paddock and ironbark tree. It fulfilled all the requirements of parent birds. Broken Beak had not worked it out in his head, but his instinct had made him select it years before.

He and his mate at that period had known what all birds know. After the eggs hatched, the young ones would be naked and helpless, needing abundant food for their growth and liable to die of exposure it left too long uncovered. It was necessary, therefore, for both the parent birds to feed the youngsters and also necessary that there should be around the nest an area big enough to supply the needs of fledglings and parents, and not trespassed upon by other food-hunting birds. It was this that caused magpies when nesting to resent the intrusion of all other birds into the selected area.

Broken Beak arrived at his ironbark tree and was vaguely disappointed to find no other magpies around. He half-expected to find a mate already installed in the tree awaiting the coming of her master, and half-hoped that some interloping male had taken over because a fight would be a fitting prelude to serious nesting business.

There still remained a few sticks of the previous season's nest, and Broken Beak told himself that these would be all the less to carry.

Perched on the highest limb of the tree, the old bird preened his feathers and then had a good look around the countryside. There was nothing of interest and not another magpie in sight, either in the air or on the ground.

This would not do.

In addition to being a fearless bird, Broken Beak was an intelligent one, and very proud of himself, notwithstanding his rather unprepossessing appearance. He had everything to offer a lady magpie desirous of setting up housekeeping—a well-stocked food paddock, an exclusive tree with the foundations of a nest already built and, of course, his valuable self. Had he been listing these attractions, he, doubtless, would have placed himself first.

Be that as it may, he considered that he had much to offer. But to whom was he to offer it? He must advertise.

And advertise he did. He had no newspapers but he did have his own glorious radio, and the four winds of heaven carried his message, poured out in those magic carolling liquid notes of which only the Australian magpie is capable. In his song he told everything—the home he wanted to build in a most desirable territory, what a magnificent fellow he was personally and what an honor it would be to any lady magpie whom he deigned to accept as a mate. The song, too, carried a warning to all other male magpies to keep away from this paddock and tree. They were Broken Beak's.

Broken Beak proved to be a first-class salesman, because within five minutes of his first broadcast, not one, but two, black and white ladies arrived, coming from opposite directions. They alighted on different branches and, after having taken stock of Broken Beak, looked each other over. The looks must have engendered mutual dislike because, without wasting time over common courtesies, they flew at each other.

Fighting clear of the ironbark tree, the two birds met in mid-air, swooping, circling and squawking, pecking, clawing and buffeting, fighting for the possession of this most eligible territory, plus Broken Beak. That dilapidated gentleman did not interfere. Not he! It was only right and proper, he thought, that these two females should battle for the right to win his favors. He left his branch and hovered over the combatants, an interesting but aloof spectator.

As far as outward appearances went, he could not tell them apart. They were both handsome black and white birds, one younger than the other; and it was the younger bird that eventually withdrew from the contest. Inexperienced in fighting, she gave way, and when almost pushed to earth by her quick-snapping antagonist, deemed discretion the better part of valor, and flapped rapidly away, leaving a few small feathers drifting on the breeze.

The contest over, Broken Beak flew back to his perch on the branch near the fork in which rested the remains of last year's nest. The victorious female did not join him immediately. Having seen her defeated rival vanish into the distance, she flew down to the ground under a stringybark tree and picked up a large twig. With this in her beak, she returned to the ironbark and, landing on the limb near Broken Beak, presented it to him. The old warrior deigned to accept it and, sidling with dignity along the limb, placed it in the old nest.

Then, without further ado, both birds flew off together in search of suitable sticks, fully to construct their future home.

Old Broken Beak's confidence in himself had been justified. He had found another mate.

Chapter II.

THE COMING OF MAGGIE.

THOUGH old Broken Beak regarded himself as an aristocrat among magpies, he was not too haughty to work. In their nest-building, his new mate found him a ready laborer and a first-class architect. Day by day the home of their future brood grew and took shape—a deep, bowl-like stick structure at the top of the ironbark tree.

At last all was ready and Broken Beak handed over complete occupancy to his mate. This did not mean, however, that he could loaf around the countryside with friends and cronies idling the time away; on the contrary, his real responsibilities had only just commenced.

In due course, four large eggs appeared in the nest. They were green-blue, with reddish-brown streaks, smears and scratches; and though it was no novelty either to Broken Beak or his mate to be the producers of such precious atoms of potential life, familiarity certainly did not breed contempt or carelessness. Broken Beak had always been a fearless and pugnacious bird, but the sight of those eggs caused such a surge of pride in his old breast that he was ready to lay down his very life if necessary in their protection.

His mate felt exactly the same about it. In between nestings she was rather a mild-mannered bird as magpies go, content to live and let live. Fearless like all her kind, she would brook no liberties or indignities, but was willing to live in peace if permitted to do so.

Gone now was that mildness of manner. With the laying of her eggs she had shed her placidity as a snake casts off its old skin. Of course, a great deal of her time now would be occupied in hatching the eggs and she would have to depend upon Broken Beak to do the major part of the guard duty; but she was more than ready to assist him if the occasion should warrant it.

In placing her reliance in her old mate, she was depending upon no broken reed. The old fellow was prepared to take on anything from a wedge-tailed eagle to a human being, large or small. He did, too, playing no favorites. Anything that came within easy radius of the ironbark tree was given tangible evidence of his battered presence.

Actually Broken Beak, like many of his species, was a more conscientious sentry than he needed to be. The paddock that contained the ironbark was not often visited by human beings, big or little, but when it was, Broken Beak swooped. He did not pause to weigh the possible consequences. It never entered his head, intelligent though he was, that these people would be ignorant of the existence of the nest if he refrained from advertising it.

He was a bird who believed in taking no chances. Every human being was a potential nest-wrecker and egg-stealer, and he took the war into the enemy's territory. He worked on the theory that though thrice is one armed who has his quarrel just, four times is that one armed who gets his blow in first. Broken Beak was a strong advocate of the military maxim that attack was the best method of defence.

Guard duty, of course, had to be interrupted in feeding his mate and keeping himself going with necessary nourishment. She used to join him occasionally, mainly for exercise, but it was not until after the eggs hatched that she left the nest for any great length of time.

With the appearance of four hungry nestlings, Broken Beak had to work overtime. It was a busy period for both parents. The youngsters had voracious appetites and the old birds were almost run off their legs and wings keeping up an adequate supply of food.

Broken Beak had been pugnacious while the eggs were in the nest, but with the advent of the youngsters he became definitely vicious. He even evolved a new plan of warfare with the assistance of his mate. Human beings entering the paddock would catch sight of Mrs. Broken Beak flying conspicuously in view having every appearance of a bird about to attack. But she never did. Her task was to keep the unwelcome visitor's attention occupied while old Broken Beak swooped unknown from behind. A swish of wings and a sharp peck was the first intimation the luckless human had of his cunning presence.

Broken Beak's plan of campaign—to attack everyone venturing near the nest and to punish the innocent with the potentially guilty—was based on the slogan that it was better to be certain than to be sorry. It was, therefore, just sheer ill-fortune that a most unusual set of circumstances brought unhappiness to him and his mate.

In an adjoining paddock there lived, in a post and rail enclosure behind a barn, a big black bull, the property of a dairy farmer named McFarlane. This bull was never permitted the wider freedom of the home paddock because it was a savage animal liable to attack man or beast if free. There had been occasions in the past that the bull had broken free and it had caused consternation in the district.

One morning the bull managed to make its escape. Continual butting and bumping against a particular rail had weakened the support until eventually it had given way. The bull soon burst out into the paddock and, after giving a triumphant bellow to announce the fact, commenced to graze around the vicinity. It was not in a particularly bad mood and as long as it was unmolested might continue to keep its temper under control.

On the other side of the paddock and behind the farmhouse, the bull's owner, blissfully ignorant of the animal's freedom, was ploughing an area of ground. Old Broken Beak observed this activity from the top of his tree, and it made him restless. He was torn between desire to do his duty in guarding the nest and desire to fly rapidly across to that ploughed ground and feed royally on the fat grubs and worms turned up by the ploughshares. He had followed ploughs before and knew of the sumptuous repasts to be had in the furrows.

From the top of his tree he could see around him for miles. All seemed peaceful and of human enemies there were none. No matter where his eyes wandered, however, they always came back to that farmer and his plough. Mrs. Broken Beak was away temporarily scouting round for food for the hungry quadruplets in the nest. When she returned, he told himself, he would take time off to venture across to the ploughed ground.

Merely thinking of the fat grubs and crickets made his

old beak water and when his mate arrived with a large caterpillar and thrust it deftly into the gaping beak of a nestling, he was ready to depart.

But here he struck a snag. His mate, who had also observed the ploughing, wanted to accompany him. They argued and squabbled about this in their own fashion, and then Broken Beak took off and flapped rapidly across the paddock, his mate closely following. They alighted together some yards behind the moving plough, dived into the furrow and, within a few seconds had completely forgotten their nest and nestlings as they hopped along, guzzling the fat white cockchafer grubs lying plentifully in the freshly-turned earth.

Back in the dairy paddock, the bull had grazed his way to the fence separating the paddock from Broken Beak's domain. Finding the top rail of one panel of fencing had fallen away, the bull stepped over the bottom and entered the magpie's territory.

In his grazing, the animal proceeded slowly in the direction of a thick clump of tea-tree and as he disappeared behind it, fate brought more actors into the drama, the climax of which would greatly annoy Broken Beak.

Scarcely had the bull disappeared behind the tea-tree scrub than three boys crawled under the fence at the far end of the paddock. One of them carried a bird trap which contained a diamond sparrow as a decoy, and their intention was to scour the bush until they found a suitable place wherein to set the trap in the hope of catching some more of those pretty little bush birds.

They had not the slightest knowledge of the magpie's

nest in the ironbark tree and possibly would never have known of its existence had the black bull stayed in its enclosure that day. Certainly, it would appear that the Fates were working against old Broken Beak. In the final analysis, it would be difficult to decide who was really to blame—the bull, or Broken Beak and his longing for a grub-feast.

The three boys, Reggie Jones, Ben Worth and Bill Thomas, had no intention of trying to trap birds in that particular paddock. Their destination was the thick bush and scrub on the other side of McFarlane's dairy farm. The paddock provided a short cut. Except for a few trees, including Broken Beak's, and the patch of tea-tree scrub behind which McFarlane's bull was now peacefully grazing, the paddock was unrelieved grassland.

Walking three abreast and talking among themselves, the boys reached the tea-tree scrub and rounded it. When they caught sight of the bull, they stopped dead and regarded it in wild surmise. The bull raised its head and looked at them. The boys returned the compliment. The bull gave a loud roar, lowered its head and began to paw the ground, sending small clods of dirt up on to its back.

That was enough for the boys. They knew the ways of bulls. Ben Worth and Bill Thomas immediately streaked for the fence, but young Jones paused long enough to pick up a huge stone, which he threw at the bull, hitting it on the head. Then, as he turned to run, he tripped over another big stone and crashed to earth. He had his wits about him, however, and when he sprang to his feet, saw he had no chance to reach the fence. Urgency lent extra strength to his already first class climbing prowess, and he had scaled the nearest tree before the bull had rushed ten yards.

From their safe position behind the fence, Ben Worth and Bill Thomas began to hurl at young Jones maledictions and advice that he did not appreciate. They pointed out to him, with what he thought was unnecessary emphasis, that he would not be in his present predicament if he had not lingered behind to throw a stone at the bull. They told him that the bull probably would not have troubled to chase them had he refrained from angering it.

"You are a first-rate idiot, Jonesy," wound up Ben Worth.

Young Jones was in no mood for censure. He was wedged in a fork of the tree while down below the bull was doing sentry-go around the trunk.

"Come and hunt this wretched hound of a thing away," he roared.

"Wretched bull of a thing, you mean," pointed out young Thomas.

"That's right, be funny!" howled Jones from the tree fork. "Don't stand there like a pair of stuffed mullets. Do something, can't you?"

"Do what?" yelled Ben.

"Come and hunt this thing away so that I can come down out of this tree!" roared Reggie. "Do you think I want to stay up here all night?"

"It's all your fault, Jonesy," called out Bill. "Who threw the stone at the bull?"

"Are you going to go through all that again?" howled young Jones. "I know I threw the stone. I know I am to blame. I know I shouldn't have done it. I know that you two have all the brains and that I'm the village idiot. I agree with everything you say. Now, will you please hunt this bull away and let me get down out of this tree?"

"How?" shouted Bill.

"I'm too big a fool to work that out. You've got all the brains, you know," replied Reggie, with a hint of sarcasm.

"Perhaps you would like me to go into the paddock and let the bull chase me, and while he is goring me to death, you can get away safely, eh?" asked Ben, who could be sarcastic too when he chose.

"Now that's what I call a great idea!" roared Reggie, eagerly. "Thanks a lot. I'll be ready. In you come!"

"Hey?" exclaimed Ben heatedly. "I'll do nothing of the kind! Who do you think you are, anyway?"

"Let me see if I can shift it," said Bill, picking up a stone and throwing it unerringly at the bull, which had stopped its sentry-go to paw up some more earth. The stone hit it on the back. It let out a bellow and rubbed its neck vigorously against the trunk of the tree.

"Stop that, for heaven's sake!" bellowed Reggie, clinging madly to a limb. "I'll get shook out of the tree, you fool!"

"Shaken out," said Bill reprovingly.

"It will save you having to climb down if you do," called out Ben, who always looked for the silver lining in the dark cloud.

Reggie's reply to both these comments was inaudible. He spluttered something most uncomplimentary, but neither Ben nor Bill could catch it.

"Listen," Reggie called out when he had got his breath

back, "Get hold of some long sticks or saplings and then come in and charge the bull as if you had rifles and bayonets. The bull won't like being charged with long sticks."

"And it won't like us for doing it, either," Ben pointed out.

Young Jones then changed his tune. He ceased reviling his two friends and began to appeal to their better natures. He mentioned that they had all been intimate pals for many years and had always helped each other. Through thick and thin they had stuck to each other, come what might, rain, hail or sunshine. Mateship was a wonderful and a precious thing.

He was speaking really well and might have gone on indefinitely in the same sentimental strain had not the bull suddenly rubbed itself vigorously against the tree trunk. Reggie ceased his exhortations and, pulling a branch off the tree, threw it down at the bull. The branch fell on the animal's horns and its efforts to dislodge the encumbrance annoyed the animal exceedingly. It roared loudly and charged the tree trunk, its head meeting it with a dull thud. The force of the impact almost threw Reggie out of the fork. He gave a startled grunt and began to climb higher.

"We have got to do something about this," said Ben to Bill. "Let us walk down the fence a bit and then enter the paddock. If we attract the bull's attention, it might chase us. We can easily get back through the fence again and Jonesy might have a chance to get clear."

"I'm willing," said Bill, and yelled out to Reggie exactly what they proposed to do. Reggie climbed down to the lower fork again and held himself in readiness to move swiftly.

Ben and Bill walked a good distance down the fence and crawled through it, advancing a few yards into the paddock. Then they started to shout loudly.

The bull, which had been watching them moving along the fence, resented the noise and, putting down its head, charged in their direction. Reggie immediately slid down the trunk to solid earth and when he reached it let out a wild, exultant cheer and began to do a species of war dance. Hearing him, the bull turned and went rushing back to the tree. Reggie made a headlong dive for the fence, realised that he could not reach it in time, so doubled back to the tree and shinned up it like a goanna, reaching the lower fork again in the very nick of time.

"Oh, you double-dyed idiot!" shouted Ben. "Why in the name of all that's stupid, couldn't you hold your silly tongue? Now we are in the same boat as before."

"The same tree fork, anyway," said Bill.

"Oh, keep quite and go home and get me a bed!" screamed Reggie. "I'm staying here for the night. I like the view."

Ben and Bill debated the matter at length and then decided to do what they should have done in the very first place—go and tell Mr. McFarlane that his bull was on the warpath.

Ben undertook the journey while Bill remained and exchanged insults with Reggie. The bull stayed beneath the tree. Ben crossed over a long way from the scene and gained McFarlane's paddock without being observed by the bull. He quickly made his way to where the farmer was ploughing and acquainted him with the news. McFarlane immediately left the plough to the magpies—Broken Beak and his mate were still there, competing with several domestic fowls for the fruits of the furrow—saddled up a horse and, whistling to his dog, cantered down to the scene of young Jones's discomfiture. He lost no time in rounding up the bull and, with the dog's aid, drove it through the broken panel of fencing and so into its own yard.

Jones was now in a position to descend the tree, but he stayed up in the fork, much to the surprise of his two friends.

"Come on down out of that tree, Jonesy," yelled Ben. "We've wasted enough time as it is because of your stupidity. It will be dark before we reach the bush, set our trap, catch some birds, and get home again."

Reggie did not reply. He stayed in the fork, glaring up towards the top of the tree. Then, to his friends' surprise, he climbed to the higher fork.

"What do you think you are, Jonesy, a blessed magpie?" Bill called out impatiently.

"No," shouted Reggie, "I don't, but there is a magpie's nest up the top of this tree and I'm going up after it."

"Better leave it alone," counselled Ben. "If the old birds see you, you'll be in for it."

"You two keep your eyes open for them. I'm going to see if there are any young ones in the nest."

Cautiously he began to climb upwards. It was fairly easy going because of the number of projecting branches, and he succeeded in reaching the fork which contained the big nest.

"Hey, Ben and Bill!" he bawled excitedly, "there are four young 'uns in it and they've got feathers. Do you want one each?"

"You bet!" cried Ben and Bill in chorus.

The four young magpies looked at the strange intruder with interest but without fear. They did not realise that they were being inspected by a representative of their greatest enemies. Indeed, one of them gave a shrill squeak and opened its beak as if expecting something to eat.

"You'll do me, maggie. You seem to have some spirit in you," Reggie told the fledgling and, seizing it with one hand, thrust it into a capacious pocket, a proceeding to which the young bird objected with an indignant but muffled squawk.

He was about to grab another when a yell from below made him change his mind.

"Get down out of that tree as fast as you can, Jonesy," roared Ben Worth. "Here comes the old birds, both of them. Hurry up, or you'll suffer for it!"

When McFarlane ceased ploughing in order to round up the bull, Broken Beak, his mate and the fowls soon disposed of all the available grubs, worms and crickets. They stayed there for a time awaiting the return of the farmer, but McFarlane did not put in an appearance. He was making sure that the bull's enclosure was secure and temporarily had forgotten the ploughing.

And it was while they were waiting for more grubs to be ploughed up that Mr. and Mrs. Broken Beak suddenly remembered their unguarded nest. Conscience-stricken and anxious, they took off from the field and flew swiftly in the direction of the ironbark tree. They were still some distance away when Ben Worth chanced to see them and shouted his warning to Reggie Jones.

Leaving the other fledglings in the nest, Reggie made his way to earth as fast as he could and joined his friends at the moment the two magpies reached their nest.

Quickly pulling the young bird from his pocket and holding its beak between his fingers to prevent it calling out, Reggie made for the dividing fence with all speed, closely followed by Ben and Bill, the latter carrying the bird trap.

They had not reached the fence before both magpies were upon them, squawking and screaming. The boys dived under the fence and made for the safety of the thick brush beyond, waving their arms above their heads and shouting to scare away the vengeful birds.

Racing through the trees, the trio reached the road and immediately crawled under a low bridge or culvert where the angry birds could not reach them. Squawking their baffled rage, Broken Beak and his mate whirled away into the sky and flew back to their ironbark home.

When Reggie and his two friends emerged from beneath the culvert and found that the coast was clear, they debated whether they should continue with their diamond sparrow trapping expedition. Reggie settled the matter as far as he, personally, was concerned, by announcing that he was going home to make a cage for his new pet.

"I'll bet your father won't let you keep it," said Ben Worth with jealousy, as young Jones stroked the fledgling's back.

"Yes he will, you'll see. Won't he, Maggie?" Reggie

asked the bird, whose sole reply was a squawk of protest. He was feeling hungry and ruffled and wanted to be back with his three brothers and sisters in the nest.

"I'm off," said his new owner. "I'll see you chaps later on. Goodbye."

"A nice sort of a friend he is," said Bill morosely, as he and Ben watched Reggie's retreating figure.

"It wouldn't have hurt him to get two more young ones while he was at the nest, would it? After all, didn't we save him from the bull? Talk about gratitude!"

"We could go back to the nest and get two more," suggested Ben.

"Yes, and who is going to climb the tree?" demanded his friend. "Not me, anyway. I'm not anxious to have my eyes pecked out. Those two old birds will be fighting mad by now. If you want a young maggie, you go and get it. I'm off home."

"I don't want any maggie," said Bill. He paused and then added with savage envy, "I hope that thing dies that Jonesy has."

"So do I," grunted Ben, and mooched off down the road, the bird trap with its chirping occupant still under his arm. That small songster was the only participant in the exciting events of the afternoon which still maintained a vestige of good humor.

Chapter III.

MAGGIE FINDS FREEDOM.

Wishful thinking prompted by jealousy had caused Ben Worth to express the opinion that Reggie Jones's father would not allow his son to keep the young magpie as a pet, but Ben's prediction almost came true. It was, however, not Reggie's father, but his mother who raised the first objection.

"I won't have that thing around this house," she told the boy when he arrived home and proudly exhibited Maggie. "You had better take it straight back and put it in its nest before your father comes home."

Ah, gee, mum, don't say that," begged young Reggie. "Maggie won't be a nuisance. I'll put him in a cage and look after him. When he grows a bit bigger we can let him run around the yard with his wing cut. He'll be as good as a watch dog and will eat all the snails and grubs and things. I'll bet dad will let me keep him."

"I'm not so sure about that," replied his mother. "I think you'll find that he will agree with me. Anyway, I don't like magpies."

"Why not, mum?"

"Because they are unlucky things to have around a house."

"Unlucky?" repeated the boy. "In what way, mum?"

"There is an Old English verse I have heard since I was

a little girl. Your grandmother used to quote it and she said it had been spoken in England for hundreds of years," said his mother. "It goes like this:

> *'I saw seven magpies in a tree,*
> *One for you, six for me;*
> *One for sorrow, two for joy,*
> *Three for a girl, four for a boy,*
> *Five for silver, six for gold,*
> *Seven for a secret that's never been told.' "*

"Where does the bad luck come in?" asked Reggie in wonder.

"One for sorrow," said Mrs. Jones. "If we have a magpie around the house trouble will come of it."

"I've never heard that poem before, but I've heard one a bit like it about pigeons," said the boy. "Anyway, mum, that poem would be about English magpies. Our teacher told us one day when we were having nature study, that the English magpie is a sort of crow and the Australian magpie is a shrike and a sort of butcher bird. They are not the same sort of birds at all."

"It's no use your arguing with me, Reggie," said Mrs. Jones sternly. "There can be no doubt about the bad luck. Your Uncle Tom once caught a young magpie and let it loose to run around his yard. He didn't have it more than two months before a visitor to his house fell over a log in the yard and broke his leg."

"The bad luck was a bit delayed, wasn't it mum?" asked the boy. "Anyway, I should think that trouble came to the visitor and not to Uncle Tom!"

"You are not being impudent, are you, my lad?" his

mother asked, regarding him sternly, and Reggie assured her fervently that he wasn't.

"We will see what your father has to say," she said finally.

If his father was likely to make him take the bird back to the ironbark tree, Reggie pondered, it would be a waste of time building a cage so, pending parental decision as to Maggie's future, the boy shut him up in a butter box with a stone on top of the lid. Reggie did not know it, but it was his mother's superstition concerning magpies that caused his father to grant him permission to keep Maggie as a caged pet. Mr. Jones had no time for superstition of any kind. He regarded as fools those people who thought certain birds were ill-omened, or thought that fortunes could be told by the stars. He did not say this to his wife when she repeated the old English poem to him and reminded him of Uncle Tom's visitor's broken leg. He was too tactful for that.

"Let the boy have his pet," said Mr. Jones. "Most boys have pets of some kind. I did when I was young. We wouldn't allow Reggie to keep a dog, you know, and it made him unhappy. A bird in a cage won't be any trouble."

"I wash my hands of the whole affair," said Mrs. Jones. "If he keeps the bird he will have to look after it. I won't."

"Gee, mum, of course I'll look after Maggie," said Reggie happily when informed of the conditions governing Maggie's retention. "I'll feed him every day on grubs and things and will always keep his cage clean."

"It looks as if the garden will be dug up by somebody else for a change," said his father.

"Yes, dad," said Reggie. "Er, mum," he added uneasily, "magpies like to eat raw meat, too."

"Do they? In that case, my lad, you will have to make friends with the butcher," said Mrs. Jones sarcastically. "Your magpie won't get any raw meat from me."

"I don't think mum likes you, Maggie," Reggie confided to his new pet some time later. The bird had now been installed in a large box with wire netting over the front, and was not enjoying the experience. Maggie was homesick for the nest in the tall ironbark and he was very, very hungry. Reggie did not think of feeding him until Maggie opened his beak wide and squawked irritably.

"I must see if I can get you some grubs," said the lad and, taking his father's spade, went down the bottom of the yard and began industriously to dig.

He soon unearthed several grubs and earthworms which he took to the cage and offered to Maggie. The young bird saw the food but did not understand that he had to take it from the boy's hand. His mother and father had always placed food straight into his beak.

He opened his bill to protest against the injustice of things and as he did, Reggie deftly dropped a grub into it. Maggie promptly gobbled it and opened his beak for more. He got them. In fact Reggie fed him grubs and worms until Maggie could hold no more. Replete, he dozed in a corner of the cage, reflecting languidly that he had never had so large a meal in so brief a period in his short life.

As the days passed, Reggie and Maggie grew quite friendly and the bird got used to the cage. He was nearly completely feathered, and had he been free, would, by now, have been learning to fly. Reggie was quite determined, when the bird was tame and friendly enough, to cut his wing and allow him to patrol the backyard. He had mentioned it to his father, but had found him unenthusiastic on the subject.

"Magpies can be nuisances when they are free like that," Mr. Jones had said. "They are liable to attack the tradespeople. If you let Maggie out and that happens, we will have to destroy him."

That had been a blow to Reggie's hopes, but he had not given up the idea. If Maggie did peck at visitors, couldn't he be put back again into his cage? There would be no need to kill him, surely! In time, Maggie learned to pick up food thrown into the cage. He gave no trouble and seemed to be content in his captivity. Even Mrs. Jones became reconciled to him when no visitors fell over objects in the backyard and broke their legs.

"That bird has a lovely voice," she remarked one night to her husband. "I heard him this morning. It was just like somebody playing a flute. Apparently he only sings in the early morning."

"That's right, mum," said Reggie, who was listening to the conversation. "He's real tame, too. I don't think it would harm anyone if he were allowed to run around the garden with his wing cut."

"I don't fancy the idea," said his father dubiously. "However, you can try it if you like. But mind what I'm telling you: if he pecks at the baker or grocer or anybody else, back he goes into his cage."

"Yes, dad," said Reggie obediently.

On the following morning, Reggie took Maggie from the cage and, with a pair of scissors, clipped the feathers of one of his wings. He then placed the bird on the ground. It was the first time in Maggie's life that he had stood on earth and he wondered what he was expected to do.

It was a strange world to him, though he had seen some of it from his cage. He had never been taught how to hunt for his own food, and since his incarceration in the cage, had never seen another magpie. He had, however, heard members of his species carolling in the early mornings.

Reggie watched him as he poked around the yard investigating everything and then a sudden thought struck the boy. He took the spade from the tool shed and, catching Maggie, took the bird down to the bottom of the yard where he was accustomed to dig worms. Placing Maggie on the ground, he got to work with the spade and soon turned up some wrigglers. Maggie's sharp eyes saw them and he immediately pounced. After that it was simple. Maggie was an intelligent bird and soon learned to connect digging with the acquisition of tasty morsels.

As the weeks passed and summer gave way to autumn and then to winter, Maggie became part of the garden and the backyard. No longer did he have to depend upon somebody digging up grubs and worms for him. He used his own sharp beak and even his claws. Lizards in the woodheap and snails among the vegetables deplored the day he was allowed out of his cage.

His one pet dislike was the baker, and it was the baker's own fault.

One morning shortly after Maggie first had been

released from his cage, the baker, entering the front gate, found the bird in his path. Maggie had no intention of molesting the bread-bringer and, therefore, was surprised and hurt when the man deliberately kicked him out of the way. Maggie did not retaliate, but hopped under the house. The baker had not kicked him out of sheer viciousness or dislike, but because he had expected Maggie to go for him. It had been the baker's experience in visiting houses that pet magpies invariably attacked him, either pecking his legs or trying to fly into his face. Therefore, when he found that the Jones family had acquired one, he decided to get in first with a self-protective kick.

And so it was his own fault that occasionally Maggie hid under the house when he was due and administered sly pecks to his heels or calves. The bird never troubled the milkman, the grocer or any other caller. Even with the baker Maggie's attacks were mild and as the bread-man did not complain to Mrs. Jones, Maggie remained free.

The family cat was not too friendly-disposed towards him, because Maggie developed the annoying habit of sneaking up behind her as she lay asleep in the sun and nipping her tail with his sharp beak.

Maggie developed several exasperating habits as the weeks rolled on. Sometimes he would sneak into the house when a door was left open, and when he did, something disappeared. It might be a thimble or some such shiny object; and one day he found a shilling lying on the floor. All these objects he hid carefully away where nobody could find them. He also rooted up young seedlings from the garden and buried them in some spot known only to himself.

It was quite useless for the Jones family to chide him about this. Maggie always wore such an innocent look. Sometimes he would lay on his back on the lawn kicking his legs and squawking like a playful dog and the family found it impossible to be angry with him.

As winter drew to a close and the warmer days of August came round. Maggie grew restless. Gradually the friendly and familiar surroundings of the house and garden became distasteful. Nothing had altered there; the change was within himself. The yard was too narrow; it seemed to be closing in upon him. He longed to be out of it—yearned to be away over the fields, the bush and the paddocks with other magpies.

The restlessness grew as the days went on and he began to hate the place. Though one of his wings had been clipped when he first was taken out of the cage and given the free run of the yard, young Reggie Jones had never troubled to keep it cut. Maggie had shown no disposition to go away, so the matter had quite slipped the boy's mind. The magpie had had a few short flights, but had never gone out of the yard itself; he had never even flown on top of the roof. There were several fruit and other trees in the garden and he had flown from one to another. It was his custom to roost in a laurel tree because it was the only tree on the Jones property that had leaves during the winter.

Early one morning, Maggie awakened to yet another day, and in the fullness of his heart greeted the rising sun with a haunting liquid flute-like melody, the like of which he had never before uttered. Something was wrong with him and he did not know what it was. It was not a physical malady, but spiritual. Maggie was a very lonely bird.

Instead of dropping from the laurel tree to the garden to search for his breakfast, he flew across to a leafless old peach tree and sat for a moment moping on a limb. Then out rang his rounded voice again in a wildly sweet song. Up, up soared the golden notes, that seemed to melt far away, and then to grow again and travel on, laden with all the sorrow of the world and all the despair of the lonely.

And as he warbled and carolled, the delightful solo became a choral-like duet. From the top of a telegraph post across the street, another magpie had joined in; but her notes were gayer and contained a hint of wonder that anyone of her kind could be sad on such a beautiful sunny morning.

Maggie ceased his song and looked around him for the other bird. All he saw was the depressing garden, the cat lying on the mat at the back door as usual, and the inevitable batch of sparrows hopping and chirping on the lawn. Maggie resented them and felt half-inclined to dash in among them and give them something serious to chirp about.

The other magpie, too, had ceased to warble, and for a moment there was quiet. Lifting his beak and pointing it at the sky, Maggie sent out a call of musical inquiry. Instantly the other magpie replied in kind and Maggie, feathers now vibrating with eagerness, flew to the highest point in the peach tree and looked around in all directions.

Then there came a rush of song from within a few yards of him. The other magpie had left the telegraph post and had alighted on the fence. She was a handsome young bird, her crisp black and white plumage glistening in the early morning sunshine.

Without pausing to think, Maggie left the peach tree and flew to the fence. The visitor looked at him approvingly as he alighted a few feet from her, and well she might, for Maggie was in splendid condition. When he sidled along the fence and rubbed his beak against her wing, she did not repulse him, but pecked the back of his head with a caressing touch that he hardly felt.

Then, without any further display, she spread her wings and flew away. Maggie looked after her in surprise and disappointment and saw her alight on the top of the telegraph post. She immediately set up a crooning song which changed to a warble and then back to a croon; and in that croon Maggie thought he detected an invitation to go and join her.

He did. It was his first long flight, but he made it easily, instinctively. He alighted on the cross-arm of the telegraph pole, but had hardly folded his wings before the tantalising female was off again, this time heading straight across country and flying rapidly.

Maggie did not wait for an invitation to follow her. Without a backward glance at the house and garden which had been his home for almost a year, he followed swiftly.

Reggie Jones had lost a pet magpie and a pet magpie had found freedom—and a mate.

Chapter IV.

THE FARMER'S FRIEND

Maggie and his new-found mate decided to build their first nest in a big gum tree on the bank of a creek which trickled through the town and wound its way through the bush beyond. The tree was in a good position and there was an adequate stretch of open field nearby for food-hunting.

They alighted in this tree and quickly approved a fork high up. And that was as far as they got in their home-planning because, before they had a chance to collect the first stick, a pugnacious, but graceful little bird, also dressed nattily in black and white, flew up to the limb on which they were sitting and told them, in a loud, shrill voice, to clear out. It was a peewit, or mudlark, and it was very angry. This tree belonged to him and his mate. They had used it for years and did not intend to surrender it to a pair of magpies, big as they were.

On a low limb of the tree—a bare limb which overhung the creek, was the peewit's nest, a big bowl of mud reinforced with grass stalks and lined with horsehair and feathers. On four reddish-white spotted eggs sat the mother bird, listening approvingly to every taunt and insult that her little mate was hurling at the magpies. It was quite true what he was saying. He and she had used this tree for some years and in between times patrolled the creek banks and the swamp a few miles away for pond snails, water beetles and any other insects they could pick up. Of course the tree was big enough to accommodate both nests, but such a thing was not done. The peewits did not want any magpies hanging around. Let them go away and find a place of their own. Goodness knows, there were enough trees in the bush!

The peewit told Maggie this and a great deal more in his shrill voice. Maggie was disconcerted by it all. So was his mate. Maggie had spent the first year of his life in a back garden and was most inexperienced. He did not know what to say to the pugnacious peewit. His mate, too, was inexperienced, and waited for Maggie to give her the lead. The magpies could easily have ignored the peewit and his wife and their pudding-basin nest, but they didn't. Rather did they feel a great deal of respect for the dapper little bird; and though the tree was a first-class one, reluctantly they decided to allow the peewit to remain in sole possession.

How Broken Beak would have despised his son for taking that attitude! If that battered old warrior had wanted this tree, he wouldn't have cared a scrap for peewit, mudlark, magpie-lark, Murray magpie, little magpie, peewee, pugwall, or whatever name it chose to go under. Broken Beak was no gentleman.

The next few days were occupied by Maggie and his mate in trying to find another tree. They were not very lucky. All the desirable ones already were occupied and their owners were more than ready to fight to retain occupancy.

In desperation, the two birds commenced to build among the wires on top of a telegraph pole. They got the nest half-built and then along came a linesman from the Postmaster-General's Department to find out what was interrupting the telephone service. He found it in the shape of some pieces of wire that Maggie had collected and twined around the 'phone wires. The linesman wasted no time in sentiment, but pulled the nest to pieces and threw it on the ground, much to Maggie's dismay. His mate who arrived with some straw as the linesman was throwing down the last few sticks, became indignant and attacked the man, buffeting him over the head with her wings while Maggie looked on in amazement. He would never, he told himself, think of attacking a human being. Humans were his friends. He had not completely forgotten the Jones family.

Maggie was to change his attitude considerably before he was much older.

They tried several times to build upon various telegraph poles but on each occasion the nest was destroyed. At length they gave it up and began to search once more for a suitable tree.

Luck favoured them at last. They found a long avenue of Moreton Bay fig trees in the park on the other side of the town and in one of these, unmolested, they built their first nest complete. They used the same tree for several nesting seasons. In the summer, autumn and winter when their broods had left the nest and were growing up, they worked the park and a paddock near it.

Death at the hands of human beings was a minor risk for the magpies during the months they were not nesting, but a number of the black and white songsters now busily foraging in the park and paddock were blissfully unaware of the narrow escape they had had from sudden extinction one early spring morning.

Maggie was to blame. It happened that, leaving the park with his mate for a short constitutional flight around the neighborhood, he discovered germinating wheat in a cultivated field. Both birds dropped down and after sampling it, found it very good. Returning to the park they foraged for ordinary fare among the grasshoppers and grubs, but the thought of those tender green shoots not half a mile away, made them dissatisfied.

In his own way, Maggie communicated his find to several of his more intimate black and white cronies, and the whole flock went over and feasted on the wheat buds.

Great was the indignation of the old farmer, Joshua Higgins, when he saw them. With loud shouts and much waving of arms, he hunted them away and they took wing scathless, except for some biting verbal comments which did them no harm at all.

Back in the park, they dismissed the angry farmer from their lives, but the farmer did not dismiss them from his. He meant to exact vengeance for the disspoiled wheat buds and next morning he was astir early and concealed himself at the wheatfield, a double-barrelled gun in his hand and anger in his heart.

After waiting a long time without sighting even one magpie, he told himself that after their scare of the previous morning, the birds were too wise to return for another meal of wheat.

He was quite wrong about it. Maggie and his friends had completely forgotten Farmer Higgins and his wheat. Something much more to their taste was engaging their attention that morning. Farmer Higgins discovered what it was as he was returning to his house to put his gun away. His neighbor was ploughing in a nearby field and there was Maggie and all his friends closely following the plough and busily gobbling the grubs and worms exposed in the furrows by the ploughshares.

When he saw Higgins leaning over the fence, young Harry Perkins stopped the plough and strolled over. He was glad of an opportunity to smoke his pipe and have a yarn.

Farmer Higgins regarded Perkins with secret scorn. The young farmer was new in the district, having been educated at an agricultural college and working his first land. Higgins, on the other hand, had been a farmer for many years, as had his father before him. He disapproved of young Perkins' scientific methods and did not favor his advanced ideas.

Perkins, too, had a lot of book learning and was always quoting figures which made the old man's head spin round.

"I've just been down hunting magpies out of my young wheat," he said. "At least, I went down to hunt them out if they were there, but they weren't. There was about a dozen yesterday picking the wheat buds and I made up my mind to shoot the lot of them today. However, I see you've got them all in your place."

"Yes," replied Perkins. "They're all friends of mine and welcome any day. I always say that the magpie is the farmer's best friend."

"Perhaps," said Higgins.

"Well, I don't mind them on my place," said the younger man, "in fact I encourage them. Presence of magpies in a crop is often an indication that caterpillars or cut-worms are attacking the roots. Magpies clear cut-worms away from lucerne, pastures and vegetables and do a wonderful job keeping down all insect pests."

"Maybe," said Higgins, thinking to himself that the young crank was preparing to give him a long lecture.

"It is a fact. The magpie is my favourite bird," said Perkins. "He gets a bit savage when nesting, but during the rest of the year is the farmer's best friend."

"You said all that before," Higgins pointed out, but the young farmer disregarded the sarcasm.

"I'll tell you this much," he said, "big battalions of magpies would be more useful than tons of poison bran for destroying grasshoppers and other insects."

"How do you make that out?" grunted Higgins.

"Simple arithmetic. If 1,000 magpies each ate 150 grasshoppers a week, they would account for 150,000. Supposing, at the lowest estimate, that each grasshopper ate a square inch of grass a day, or seven square inches a week, those 1,000 magpies would save the farmer 1,050,000 square inches of grass a week for his stock."

"It sounds all right as you say it," said Higgins, "but grasshoppers come in millions, not thousands."

"Only country people know the value of our native birds in combating the enemies of our crops," went on young Perkins. "Children at school are taught to be kind to birds and most of them join the Gould League of Bird Lovers; but with some of them it just goes in one ear and out of the other, especially city children. Of course the only birds they see are at the zoo or in the city parks.

"And talking about that," he said, "I've seen people in

the city parks feeding battalions of sparrows with crumbs from their lunches. Those parks seem to be the rendezvous for all the useless birds living—sparrows, starlings, Indian turtle doves, bulbuls and so on. They are just a lot of imported pests, yet city people encourage them by feeding them with their lunches. I'd like to feed them with a double-barrelled shotgun!"

"Who, the city people?" ejaculated Higgins.

"No," laughed Perkins, "the city sparrows and starlings."

"Well, the more they have in the city parks, the less there are for us to worry over in the country," said Higgins.

"There is something in that," mused Perkins. "Still, the fact remains that a lot of city folk think that we in the country are a lot of cranks and not quite right in the head for wanting to protect birds."

Higgins told himself that there was one crank in the country anyway, but he did not say it out aloud.

"Take magpies," said the young farmer. "If they attack people in the parks the police shoot them on the spot. Shoot the magpies, I mean, not the people," he added quickly.

"Magpies don't have much chance to do good in the city."

"Haven't they!" exclaimed Perkins. "What about the worms and crickets they destroy on bowling greens and golf courses?"

"I know you think I'm a bit of a bore on this subject of birds, Mr. Higgins," he went on after a short pause to light his pipe. "Possibly I am, but facts and figures taught me at the agricultural college have made me that way. Take the plague locusts. Every year millions and millions of them sweep Australia eating the heart out of the country, leaving behind them starving stock and damage running into millions of pounds."

"Grasshoppers do the most damage," said Higgins.

"That is what I am talking about. People will insist on calling the things grasshoppers when they age really plague locusts. Any scientist will tell you that.

"Anyway," he went on, "what's in a name? What does it matter what they are called? It doesn't prevent them doing the damage. I'm convinced that a lot of the trouble is due to the fact that we haven't enough native birds to stop these locusts breeding into plague proportions. There is far too much slaughter among our native birds by poison, pests and people. Rabbit and grasshopper poison, crow traps, foxes, dingoes, wild cats, eagles, hawks and unthinking human beings are slowly but surely denuding Australia of her most beautiful and valuable birds."

"You can't tell me that birds can stop a grasshopper plague," protested Higgins. "There are not enough birds in the world to do that."

"No, but if the birds had been protected properly from the very early days, the hoppers would never have reached plague proportions," said Perkins. "I've examined grasshopper or plague locust laying grounds and the things lay so close together that they average 10,000 eggs to a square foot of ground. This makes over 400,000,000 eggs to the acre. Think of that, man! What chance would any of us farmers have of survival if the grasshoppers did not have plenty of enemies, including magpies.

"You've got to remember, too, that this plague locust is

at work all the year round, though, thank goodness there is not a continuous swarm of them. The eggs laid in winter hatch out about September and this crowd lays eggs round about January or February. The lot hatched from these lay theirs in May and so the cycle goes on and on. It is only during spring that they reach plague numbers."

"I've never taken much personal interest in the origin of the things," confessed Higgins. "It is bad enough just knowing that they are in existence and that we can expect them by the million every September and October and November. However, there might be something in what you say about the shortage of birds."

"There is," said the young farmer earnestly. "And the whole point is that the greatest pests we have are not Australian birds at all, but imported rubbish. Did you know that?"

"Never given it a thought," replied Higgins. "Birds are just birds to me. Some of them I like and some of them I hate. My special hate is the starling. What possible use is that thing?"

"That proves my point," said Perkins. "Starlings are not native Australians and neither are those other pests, the sparrows and turtle doves."

"Sparrows and starlings come from Europe and Asia," said Perkins. "Starlings are really filthy birds and definitely the most noxious of all the imported feathered rubbish. They build their nests in houses and those nests are the breeding grounds for vermin. They eat like anything and breed very fast. Don't they make a mess of fruit trees, strawberry patches and vegetables, too? I had most of my young lettuce cleaned out by a flock of starlings."

"So did I," said Higgins. "Yet I've seen starlings eating grasshoppers and other insects."

"They do, but the damage they inflict on crops and fruit far outweighs the good they accomplish eating a few insects. What I've got against them also is the fact that they attack small useful insect-eating birds and pass vermin on to them. I've known little birds to lose all their feathers through this."

"How did the things get out here in the first place?" asked old Higgins, growing interested in spite of himself.

"I learned all about that at the college," said Perkins with a smile, and Higgins inwardly reproached himself again for giving the young man a fresh lead. "It isn't certain when the first lot arrived from Europe, but there are records of a shipment in 1863 when the ship "Princess Royal" landed a cargo of starlings and sparrows in Melbourne. They were actually sold in the markets at high prices."

"Hey? Sold in the markets?" ejaculated the astonished Higgins.

"Yes. Another ship, the "Orient," brought out a load of 100 sparrows from England in the same year, but only one, a cock bird, survived the trip."

He broke off and grinned.

"Guess how much they sold him for," he said. "Sold him? About twopence, I'd say," guessed Higgins.

"Twopence? Eleven shillings, you mean!" said Perkins, and the old farmer gasped.

"You're pulling my leg, Perkins," he said.

"That's history," said Perkins soberly. "Curious, eh? The same ship brought out another cargo of sparrows in

1865 and these were handed over to the Botanical Gardens. I suppose they thought the things would cheer the place up. There are millions of them now over most of Australia, though Western Australia so far has managed to keep them out. They can't cross the arid Nullabor Plains and desert. Awful pests they are, choking up gutters with their nests and destroying fruit and vegetables."

"You're right there," said Higgins.

"Birds are not the only imported pests we farmers have to put up with," said Perkins, "Look at the rabbits. They brought some of them out with Governor Phillip in the first fleet in 1788, placed them in a special enclosure with a gamekeeper to feed them and look after them. In those days they fenced rabbits in and paid a man to care for them. Since then the public has spent thousands of pounds on fences to keep them out. Then there is the fox. A hunt club in Victoria imported them in the early days so that the gentry could go fox hunting for sport. Now the things have spread throughout the Commonwealth and do thousands of pounds worth of damage killing lambs, poultry and nesting native birds."

"Yes," said Farmer Higgins vaguely. "I guess you are right. Ah, well, I must be getting up to the house for dinner. I'll see you later on. Give my love to the magpies. Good day."

"Cheerio," replied Perkins, and returned to his plough. Maggie and his friends were still there, patiently awaiting his return because they had cleaned up all the worms and grubs available.

"Giddap," commanded the young farmer, and the placid old plough horses responded immediately, the shares turning the rich brown earth and exposing bigger and better grubs for the delectation of the sharp-eyed magpies.

Maggie changed his mind about the goodness of human beings that nesting season. A boy climbed the fig tree and tried to steal the eggs from the nest under Maggie's very eyes. His mate had been away taking a little exercise, leaving him to guard the nest. He was in the fig tree and saw the boy climbing it, but thought nothing of it. He did not suspect that the lad had designs on the eggs.

It was when the youngster actually reached the nest and began to pick the eggs up that Maggie realised what was going on. All his respect for the human race, instilled in him when he was the pet of the Jones family, fell from him in a flash and he became a fury—the true son of old Broken Beak, that warrior who hated humans like poison.

Maggie flew at that boy and pecked him on the head. Then he whirled away for another strike and, flying down, beat his wings in the lad's face, almost blinding him. The boy began to howl and slid down the tree to the ground as fast as he could. Unfortunately he missed his grasp before he could make it, and fell the last twenty feet, breaking his arm on the rock-like ground.

There was a great deal of unpleasantness over that episode. The boy was picked up and taken away, and some time later several men arrived at the tree. They had a rifle and with it took pot shots at Maggie and his mate. They did not harm either bird, but they did damage the nest, breaking two of the eggs. However, the other two hatched out and the fledglings grew unmolested.

Maggie and his mate, nesting over for that year, took

their latest family to the hunting park and paddock and taught them the usual things. There were only a dozen birds working these areas and Maggie's twins easily fitted in for a time. When August came round the two youngsters would, in the ordinary course of events, find their own mates and leave to set up housekeeping in some other district.

And this duly occurred.

Chapter V.

TROUBLE AHEAD

WITH the nesting season at hand once more, Maggie and his mate left the park one bright morning in late winter and decided to establish their new home in a high gum tree which grew in a paddock on the outskirts of the town.

Maggie had keen memories of the previous spring and summer and, being an intelligent bird and wise now in the ways of juvenile humans, resolved to avoid a repetition. He had given humans only a passing thought since his last brood had grown up. He had seen plenty of them, but they had not interfered with him and he had had no cause to interfere with them.

Nest-building proceeded without incident and in the course of time the deep, bowl-shaped nest of sticks held four eggs. Regarding them with a jealous eye, Maggie prepared to defend them by every means in his power. Woe betide any prowling climbing animals that sought to despoil that nest! Woe betide any creature of the air which dared even to perch in that tree. Above all, let all thieving human boys doubly beware! None of them would get the chance to climb the tree while Maggie was on guard.

Adventures were few for the guardians of the nest during the days that followed the appearance of the last of the eggs. On one occasion Maggie thought it necessary to swoop down upon a man who ventured near the tree. The man did not know that there was a magpie's nest within twenty miles, and his astonishment was great when the black and white feathered bullet hit his hat, knocking it to the ground. Maggie whirled aloft again with a shrill squawk of hate, ready to charge a second time if necessary, but the man left the vicinity with some haste.

Only two young ones were hatched from the eggs and Maggie and his mate were kept busy satisfying their voracious appetites.

They had no further tilts with humans until one afternoon when, perched on a limb above the nest with his mate, Maggie noticed a boy emerge from the bushes across the way and come to a halt under a big tree some hundreds of yards away. Before the boy's arrival, Maggie had been interested in that tree. Always on the look out for something with which to feed his hungry children, he had noticed hundreds of insects flying around the tree. Investigations had shown them to be bees, and Maggie had returned to his own tree in disgust. He did not like bees, either personally or as food.

As he watched the boy standing under the tree, Maggie noticed that he had a large bright object in one hand and big stick in the other. He placed the bright object on the ground. It was a kerosene tin and though Maggie did not know what it was, he had seen such things in the Jones' back yard. From the tin the boy took a queer looking object which appeared to have a long beak. It was a small bellows, but Maggie had never seen such a thing before. The boy placed this on the ground and then took up the kerosene tin again.

Suddenly the still afternoon air was shattered by a series of loud, banging noises. The boy was energetically hitting the kerosene tin with the stick. Now why on earth was that mad human doing such a ridiculous thing?

As Maggie pondered the point, out of the bushes came two more boys, and the magpie felt his temper rising. Boys meant trouble. But, thought Maggie, as he was on the point of launching himself at them, obviously these boys were not interested in his nest—at least not yet. It was quite apparent that something in the other tree was claiming their undivided attention. What could it be? Not another nest, because Maggie knew his was the only one in those parts.

Jacky Peters, who was so energetically banging the kerosene tin, was interested in those very bees that Maggie earlier had rejected as food, and he was not pleased with the arrival of the other two boys, Fred Neville and Harry Butt.

"After them there bees, Jacky?" inquired young Butt, whose nickname, owing to his disposition, was "Happy."

"No, chasing rainbows," retorted Jacky, who often mishandled the truth.

"What are you making all that row with the kerosene tin for?" demanded Fred Neville, a freckled-faced youngster with a hole in his pants, to whom his friends had applied the somewhat unattractive nickname of "Nibbler."

"Because I want to be the drummer in the school band," retorted Jacky. "I'm just having some quiet practice."

Nibbler was puzzled.

"But the school ain't got no band, Jacky," he said. Nibbler never won any prizes for grammar.

"He thinks that the bees will like the music and follow

him home so that he can put them in a hive," said Happy with a grin.

Jacky Peters put down the kerosene tin.

"Listen to me, you two," he said. "I'm after that swarm of bees in that tree and I don't want any foolishness from you, see? If you want to know why I'm banging this tin, it is to make the bees swarm. They are following their queen by the noise she makes and when I bang the tin they can't hear her, so they all settle in a swarm."

"Go on! Is that so?" asked the interested Nibbler.

"No it isn't," put in Happy. "It's only a tale. I've heard that before and it doesn't make bees swarm at all. Don't you believe him, Nibbler."

"It is so, I tell you!" roared Jacky.

"You might think it is," said Happy, "but that doesn't alter the fact that it is all rot."

"Do you want a punch in the eye, Happy?" demanded Jacky belligerently. "If so, you're going the right way to get one."

"All right, all right, I'm sorry," said Happy soothingly. He did not want to fall out with Jacky Peters who was the best fighter in the school.

"What is that thing that looks like a pair of bellows?" asked Nibbler, pointing to the object that Jacky previously has taken from the kerosene tin.

"It's a smoking outfit that us bee men use," said Jacky in superior tones. "You put some stuff in that hole on top and light it and then you can squirt smoke on the bees to make them keep quiet."

"Go on!" said Nibbler, impressed. Happy merely sneered silently.

"How are you gonna get the bees, anyway?" asked Nibbler. "I see most of them have settled on a big branch up the tree."

"Didn't I tell you?" exclaimed the triumphant Jacky. "They are in an awkward place, though. I wish they had settled close to the ground or on a low bush."

"Well, supposing I climb the tree and knock them off with a stick. Will you catch them?" asked Happy, who intended to knock the bees over Jacky if he had a chance and make that lad look silly.

Happy forgot that bees were not nice insects to play around with.

"All right, but don't go hurting the queen," warned Jacky.

"How will I know the queen? Will she have a crown on her head?" asked Happy, desiring to infuse a little light and laughter into the conversation.

"Climb the tree if you are going to, and don't try to be so funny, Happy," snorted Jacky, who was not feeling humorous.

With much gasping and grunting, Happy negotiated the trunk and eventually reached the same branch on which the bees were hanging in a compact mass. He climbed out as far as he could, getting to within a yard or two of the swarm.

"Hey, down there!" he called out to Jacky, who was watching his progress with interest, "I forgot to bring a stick up with me."

"Well pull one off the tree itself," instructed Jacky. He stepped backwards to get a better view and almost fell over Nibbler, who was taking time off from bee-watching to pelt pebbles at a frog in a nearby waterhole.

In breaking a long twig from the tree, Happy disturbed the bees, several of which made for him. With angry insects buzzing around him, he slid rapidly to earth and immediately rushed away through the scrub, the bees and Jacky after him. Nibbler stayed where he was.

"Keep still, you fool, and they won't sting you!" shouted Jacky. "Let them settle on you and then I'll get them."

The rapidly-retreating Happy paid not the slightest heed to this rather selfish advice but kept on going.

High up in his gum tree, Maggie watched the quickly changing scene with amazement. What on earth could those silly humans be doing?

After making a circuit of a large tract of bushland, the howling Happy returned to his starting point. He made a headlong dash for the waterhole, crashed into Nibbler who was now trying to get the frog by spearing at it with a long stick, and sent him headfirst into the muddy water. Happy Butt had never been noted for his love of water, but he took to that unattractive pond with headlong dash, leaping into it on top of the screaming Nibbler.

Bees floated on the surface, but the main swarm had already deserted the tree—and his person—for a nearby prickly bush.

Jacky stood on the bank and looked anxiously at Happy.

"Is the queen on you anywhere?" he asked.

"Never mind the silly queen," howled Happy, delicately removing wet bees from his hair, "I'm wet and stung to death."

"Me too," screamed the ungrammatical Nibbler,

flopping around in the muddy water. "I'll tell me mother on you, Happy."

Moaning loudly, the unhappy Happy dragged himself ashore. Jacky inspected him carefully, but could see no bees, queens or commoners. Happy as a carrier of bees was important, but Happy without bees had no value in Jacky's eyes, so he made for the prickly bush. Nibbler, losing all interest in the frog, which was regarding him scornfully from the shelter of a bunch of reed, also crawled ashore and there they stood a wet and sorrowful pair.

"I'm gonna tell me mother…" began Nibbler, but what information he intended to convey to her will never be known, because his remarks were cut short by a backhander from Happy. Poor Nibbler gave just one soul-shaking sob and shut up.

Meanwhile, Jacky was doing wonderful things with his smoking outfit. He had placed a black veil over his face, which made him look like a hooded terror, and was squirting smoke on the swarm of bees. Happy, growing a little interested, and forgetting temporarily the three bee stings he had collected, went up and peered over his shoulder. A discontented bee settled on the back of his neck and then stung him.

Happy, already a little over-wrought, made a whack at the back of his neck and, in doing so, quite inadvertently dug his elbow into Jacky's ribs. Jacky gave a grunt of surprise and dropped the smoking outfit. The bees got restless and showed signs of moving. One stung Nibbler on the back of the hand.

"Oh, my heavens." he cried, in heart-tending tones.

Jacky was annoyed.

"Look, you two," he said shortly, "clear off and let me get these bees in peace. Go on, get going!"

Saying which, he deliberately kicked Happy on the calf of the leg. Happy, in anguish, turned on him like an insane tiger.

"Take that!" he howled, and punched Jacky right between the eyes. Such a blow, delivered to the best fighter in the school, could have but one effect, and within seconds Jacky and Happy were fighting furiously. Then Nibbler got excited. Being on Happy's side he sought to assist his friend by kicking Jacky. Jacky swung round on him and hit him on the chest with such force that Nibbler went head over heels. This diversion gave Happy his opportunity and he punched Jacky vigorously on the chin. Jacky sank to the ground, knocked out.

"Get up and have some more," panted Happy, dancing around the prostrate lad. Jacky made no reply.

"You've killed him, Happy," said Nibbler, horror-stricken.

"Don't be mad!" said Happy, calming down and beginning to feel scared. He did not think he had killed Jacky, but he feared for his safety if that lad recovered suddenly.

"Come on, let us get away from here while our luck is in," advised the trembling Nibbler.

"But we can't leave him lying there like that," protested Happy.

"I can anyway," said Nibbler and, without further ado, took to his heels. Happy lingered for a few seconds and then too departed hurriedly.

Up in his tree, Maggie had followed everything with

intense interest, and the sight of the quiet body on the ground proved too much for his inquisitive nature. Silently he volplaned down and landed within a few feet of Jacky's head. With his own head inquisitively on one side, he studied the boy carefully. Then he hopped a little closer. Jacky reminded him vaguely of his friend, Reggie Jones.

And this was the scene that burst upon the gaze of Jacky Peter's father, who, crossing the bush track, as he sometimes did on his way home from work found his son lying unconscious on the ground with a magpie guarding him.

As the man approached, Maggie quickly took to his wings, flying to a branch above. Mr. Peters tenderly raised his son's head and when he did, saw blood on the back of the scalp. In falling, Jacky had hit his head on a piece of stone hidden in the grass, but his father did not know this.

"What's wrong, Jacky? Are you badly hurt?" asked the anxious father, sitting on the ground and pillowing the boy's head on his lap. "What happened?"

Jacky gave a low moan and opened his eyes slowly. His head was aching a lot. Recognising his father, he said weakly, "Hullo, dad."

"What happened, Jacky?" repeated his father. "Have you had an accident or been in a fight?"

Jacky had had an accident all right—a horrible accident. He, the champion fighter of the school, had been beaten in a fight. It would not bear thinking about. He closed his eyes again and groaned.

"Did that magpie attack you son?" asked Mr. Peters. "There is a wound on the back of your head. Did that bird do it?"

Jacky, whose senses were clearing rapidly, wondered what his father was talking about.

"Magpie? What magpie, dad?" he asked vaguely.

"When I came along just now and saw you lying on the ground, there was a magpie standing here near your head," his father explained. "This is the nesting season and they are very vicious just now. Did that one pick a hole in your head?"

Jacky thought rapidly. Here was a golden opportunity to save his reputation as a fighter.

"I really don't know what happened, dad," he said slowly. "I was out here looking for a swarm of bees and was standing near this tree when something hit me on the back of the head. I know nothing more about it. It might have been a magpie."

"Of course it was!" exclaimed his father. "The thing must have struck you with such force that you fell over. You might have bumped your head on the ground too, but undoubtedly the magpie is the cause of the trouble. Why, I can see the mark of the thing's beak on your head!"

Jacky paid silent tribute to his father's imagination, but did not comment openly.

"I'll see the police about this," said Mr. Peters harshly. "I'll have the bird shot. He must have a nest around here. I've never liked magpies and I'll see that there is one less in this town!"

"Yes, dad," said Jacky.

"Let me help you up and take you home, son," said his father. "I'll go to the police station as soon as I get you to the house."

As he accompanied his father along the road, Jacky's

thoughts were racing. He must get hold of Happy and Nibbler and tell them the mistake his father had made. He would get them to back up his story and then the news of the fight would not come out. No; the better course would be to swear them to secrecy. Perhaps he could scare them into keeping silent as to what actually had occurred by saying that his father would tell their parents they had attacked him.

The main thing, Jacky considered, was that his fighting reputation had to be maintained at all costs. At present he was cock of the walk at school. If the other boys learned that he had been beaten in a fight by Happy Butt, a second rate fighter at any time, his reign would be over.

Jacky shuddered. The idea of that appalled him.

Chapter VI

DEATH IN THE TREES

True to his word, Mr. Peters, immediately he had concluded his evening meal, paid a visit to the police station. Jacky did not go with him. He pleaded a sore head, but the real reason for his staying at home was that he did not have the courage to face wise old Sergeant Grant. He knew that astute police officer would see through his story in no time.

When Mr. Peters made his complaint to the sergeant, the officer smiled.

"That boy of yours has been pulling your leg, Mr. Peters," he said, and when Mr. Peters demanded that the officer go and shoot the magpie at the earliest possible moment, Sergeant Grant refused point blank.

"I can't go shooting protected birds indiscriminately," he protested. "You have absolutely no proof that young Jacky was attacked by a magpie. He doesn't even say so himself, from what you tell me."

"Because he didn't see it, but he felt it. I saw the bird on the ground looking at him and I wouldn't be surprised if the thing pecked him while he was lying unconscious. One thing is certain. The boy had a wound on the back of his head."

"Perhaps he got into a fight and was knocked down," suggested Sergeant Grant.

"There is no boy in this town capable of knocking him down," retorted Mr. Peters with pride. "Anyway, if he had been in a fight he would have told me."

"Not if he had been knocked out. Perhaps he met his match and didn't like to say so," said the shrewd old sergeant, but Mr. Peters dismissed that preposterous suggestion scornfully.

"The magpie attacked the boy and that's flat. Are you going to shoot it, or aren't you? That's all I want to know."

"I am not," said the sergeant.

"Then must I myself do the work you are paid to do?" demanded the angry father, and Sergeant Grant looked at him sternly.

"Now Mr. Peters, I wouldn't do anything rash if I were you," he warned. "Magpies are protected by law and anybody who kills them without permission is liable to a very heavy fine."

"Do you mean to sit there and tell me that those vicious things are protected and that people are not allowed to kill them?" shouted Mr. Peters. "Have we got to put up with the risk of having our eyes picked out and be prevented from doing anything about it?"

"I didn't make the law, Mr. Peters, but it is my job to see that it is observed," said the sergeant patiently. "Magpies are vicious at this time of the year because they are nesting and protecting their nests and young ones. No matter what you say, the position is quite plain. It is an offence for any person to shoot a magpie unless permission to do so is given by the police after it has been proved that a bird is a danger to the community."

"Very well then. If you won't shoot the thing yourself, will you give me permission to do so?"

"No I won't," said Sergeant Grant. "In the first place, I've had no other complaints about this particular bird, and in the second place, speaking quite frankly, I don't believe this story of your son's."

"It is only partly his story and partly mine," said Mr. Peters.

"I still don't believe it."

"You infer that my boy Jacky is telling lies, eh?" exclaimed Mr. Peters. "Jacky is an honest, straightforward, decent lad, and it is a pity all the lads in this town are not like him."

Sergeant Grant looked at him quizzically.

"I'm glad they are not; otherwise my job would be doubly difficult," he said. "I'm not calling him a liar, but I'm not endorsing all the fine things you have said about him.

"Mr. Peters," went on the old sergeant quietly, "you know as well as I do that that boy of yours is at the bottom of most of the mischief in this town. He is a thorough-paced young rip. Who was it who collected a box full of mice and allowed them to go loose in the picture theatre? That almost caused a riot and nearly frightened several old ladies to death. Who was it that took a tin of red paint and slapped it all over the backs of those prize white leghorn hens that Mr. Sylvester intended entering in the poultry show?"

"All boys play jokes," grunted Mr. Peters. "There is no harm in the boy."

"Jokes, you call them?" snorted Sergeant Grant. "I have

a sense of humour, I hope, but I couldn't see anything funny in those two episodes—two among many. No, Mr. Peters, you'll have to bring me better proof of the viciousness of this magpie than that supplied by your son."

When Jacky's father returned home in a great rage and reported the conversation to the boy, Jacky felt a little uneasy. His father, however, did not question him further on the details of the occurrence in the paddock. His wrath was divided equally between Sergeant Grant and Maggie and he told Jacky that he fully intended to take the law into his own hands and shoot Maggie on the following afternoon. Jacky resolved to have a talk with Happy and Nibbler as quickly as possible.

He interviewed his youthful acquaintances on the following morning. It was a Saturday and he found them both in the park. Happy looked wary as Jacky approached and was prepared for hostilities. Being honest with himself, he realised that, in beating Jacky in the fight on the previous afternoon, he had been assisted by luck and by young Nibbler. He doubted very much whether he could beat Jacky in a stand-up contest with fists.

He was, therefore, very much on the alert as Jacky approached. He did not want to fight if he could avoid it, and he hoped that Jacky had forgotten the distressing affair. Jacky's first words dispelled that faint hope.

"About yesterday," he commenced, facing Happy squarely.

"Well, what about?" asked Happy, more wary now than ever.

"Do you know what happened to me after I fell over during the fight?"

"No, what did happen?" asked Happy. He was discreet enough not to point out that Jacky had been knocked down by a fist and had not fallen over at all.

"I hit my head on a stone and the doctor thinks it might turn out something bad," said Jacky, drawing on his imagination.

"Why should it drive you mad?" asked Nibbler, who had not quite heard what Jacky had said.

"Bad, not mad!" snorted Jacky. "My father found me and took me home and he is looking for the fellows who knocked me down. He went to the police last night."

"The police?" breathed Happy uneasily, while Nibbler looked scared.

"Yes, the police," repeated Jacky, pleased with the impression he had made. "If the police can get hold of the fellows who attacked me they will go to gaol."

"Go to gaol," repeated Happy mechanically.

"That's what I said. Go to gaol. Maybe for about ten years, too," said Jacky, again drawing on his vivid imagination.

"T-t-ten-y-y-years!" stuttered Nibbler. "T-t-that's a p-p-pretty long t-t-time."

"A very long time. You and Happy will be men before you come out," said Jacky ominously.

Nibbler thought he saw a bright spot.

"It was Happy who belted you, not me," he said. "So they'll only take Happy to gaol. I'm safe!"

"Nobody belted me, Nibbler!" exclaimed Jacky. "And don't think you can get out of it. The police know I'm the best fighter in this town and that it would take more than one fellow to knock—er, I mean, make me fall down."

"Just a minute," cried Happy. "Do you mean to say that you told your father and the police about the fight? Why, you tale-bearer and tittle-tat! It was just a bit of a fight like all boys have now and then."

"I didn't say I told who did it," said Jacky slowly. "As a matter of fact, I haven't told them yet. I said I didn't know who did it but might be able to find out."

"Now just you listen to me for a minute, Jacky Peters," said Happy, whose intellect had been sharpened by the instinct of self-preservation and the passionate desire to avoid serving ten years in prison.

"What is all this coming to? I knocked you down and you know I knocked you down. Your father and the police, you say, are looking for the fellow who knocked you down. Why haven't you told them?

"And don't try to tell me you have kept your mouth closed because you do not like carrying tales, because I won't believe you, see?" he added rapidly as Jacky opened his mouth to say something. "Just tell me plainly what is at the back of all this. What do you want from us to make you keep your mouth shut? You want something, don't you, eh?"

Jacky was rather taken aback by the clear language in which Happy had stated the case.

"Why I, er, don't know what you mean, Happy," he began vaguely; but Happy cut him short.

"I've got your measure, Jacky," he said. "Better speak out plainly and save time."

"All right then, Happy, I will," said Jacky. "We had a fight yesterday and you and Nibbler knocked me down. You couldn't have done it on your own. Now, before I go any further, how many kids have you told about it?"

"None," said Happy.

"What about you, Nibbler?"

"None, neither," said Nibbler.

"Why haven't you?" demanded Jacky. "Why haven't you both gone around boasting and bragging about how you knocked down the best fighter in the school?"

"For one thing, I haven't had the time," said Happy honestly. "When I got home last night I got into an awful row about having mud all over my clothes and I was too sore with a couple of bee stings to think about anything else."

"Nor me neither," said the ungrammatical Nibbler. "I got a good hiding too."

Jacky had two aims—the preservation of his fighting reputation and the destruction of the magpie. He knew that his father would attempt to shoot the bird that afternoon and he knew, too, that if Sergeant Grant found this out, and he was sure to, Mr. Peters might get into serious trouble. It was to save his father from that risk, and himself from the resultant parental wrath if the truth ever came out, that he had resolved to kill Maggie himself.

He intended to try to make Happy and Nibbler help him.

"Happy," he said at last, "I really ought to give you a good hiding over yesterday, but I'll forget all about it if you'll forget all about it too. That goes for you also, young Nibbler," he added, turning a fierce eye on the school's worst grammarian.

"I'm willing to forget all about it, Jacky," said Happy, "but just what is it going to cost me?"

Happy, it will be seen, had small faith in the generosity and forgiveness of Master Peters.

"Practically nothing," replied Jacky. "I just want you and young Nibbler to help me get a couple of young magpies from a nest."

"And where is this nest?"

"Down in a tree just near where we had the fight."

"I didn't know there was a magpie's nest there."

"I'm not sure exactly where it is," said Jacky, "but after you two ran away yesterday, my father and I were tackled by a magpie. It must have a nest there somewhere."

"And you want me and Nibbler to go down there and get our eyes picked out by a magpie while you get the young ones, do you?" said Happy with some heat. "You've got a hide like a brick wall."

"Thicker than that," said Nibbler.

"You hold your tongue, Nibbler, or I'll give you a black eye," said Jacky with a frown; and Nibbler, who had no use for a black eye, decided to remain silent.

"I see it all now," said Happy resentfully. "I knew you wanted something out of me. Didn't I say he'd want something out of me, Nibbler?"

"You did, too," said Nibbler.

"All I want you and Nibbler to do," said Jacky patiently, "is to come down to the tree with your catapults and stand guard ready to hunt the old birds away while I climb the tree. I'm not asking you to climb it, am I?"

"Not yet, you haven't, and if you did ask, it would be a waste of time," snorted Happy.

Jacky was satisfied with the way things were shaping.

Happy really thought that the price of silence was his assistance in getting a young magpie from a nest. Jacky had, of course, no intention of climbing the tree if he found a nest. All he wanted was some assistance in killing the parent bird.

"Listen, I'm not asking you to take any risks," he said soothingly. "You and young Nibbler can use your catapults on the old birds if necessary. I'll do all the hard work. What do you say?"

"No," said Happy.

"No, too," said Nibbler.

"Very well, then, we'll say no more about it," said Jacky. "Goodbye, I must be moving. I've got to go to the police station. I want to tell Sergeant Grant all about yesterday."

"With a lot of additions too," said Happy bitterly. "If you go to the police station, Nibbler and I will tell all the kids how I knocked you out—with additions."

"You won't have much chance in gaol," said Jacky coldly.

"For ten years," faltered Nibbler.

"Probably more," said the relentless Jacky.

"It's all rubbish. They wouldn't put a boy in gaol for ten years for having a fight," said Happy, but his tones showed that he had his doubts about that.

"Have a bit of sense and don't take the risk," said Jacky cunningly.

Happy pondered the matter intensely for some seconds and then sighed heavily.

"Come on," he said, "let's get down to the paddock and see if we can find this magpie's nest."

With the elated Jacky leading the way, the three boys marched off. They paused at the side of the road to fill their pockets with suitable pebbles for their catapults, and then continued on to the paddock, walking one behind the other like three Indians on the war trail. When they reached the rather dense scrub that ringed the clearing in which stood the gum tree in which the bees had swarmed, Jacky motioned his two companions to a halt.

"Let us have a look around first before we go out into the open," he said. "There are only three or four trees here and I'm sure the nest isn't in the one where the bees were. Have a good look at the rest."

Standing in the scrub and feeling somewhat like three pioneers keeping a watch out for wild aboriginals, the boys subjected the high branches of the various trees to a careful examination.

"Can't see a thing," said Happy. "I don't think there is a nest here. I can't see any magpies around either."

"I can!" exclaimed Nibbler suddenly. "Look, there's one flying into the tree over there!"

Looking eagerly in the direction indicated, Happy and Jackie saw a magpie disappear among the thick foliage at the top of the tree and a few seconds later they heard the excited squawking of the hungry fledglings.

"What did I tell you!" cried Jacky. "Look, there goes the old bird off again for some more food. Now is our chance."

"Our chance for what?" asked Happy coldly. "It's your chance, you mean. I'm stopping here with Nibbler."

"Come on in a bit closer," urged Jacky. "You can't keep a proper watch from here. Anyway, the old bird had gone. Come on. Don't be such a pair of cowards."

He stepped into the clearing, his catapult pouch loaded with a stone and his eyes alert for the first sign of the returning magpie. Happy and Nibbler followed him reluctantly, their catapults also at the ready.

It was quite true that a parent bird was away foraging for food, but it wasn't Maggie. That black and white songster was perched on a limb of the tree between that which contained his nest and that in which the bees had been. He was watching the trio with hate-filled eyes. These boys were his hereditary enemies and he knew from the things they carried that they were up to no good.

Maggie watched them walking towards the tree in which his nest was built and as they reached the bottom of the trunk, he spread his wings and hurtled down, his sharp beak pointed rigidly at the back of Happy's neck. There was a flurry of wings and a savage squawk and Maggie was high in the air again.

But Happy's cap was lying on the ground and Happy was yelling wildly and rubbing his right ear which the bird's pointed beak had furrowed as if a nail had been scratched across it.

Down plunged the irate Maggie again. Jacky raised his catapult, but in the excitement of the moment, sent the stone wide. Maggie misjudged the dive and crashed on to Nibbler's shoulder, his wings brushing that startled youngster's cheek and his claws scratching his neck.

Nibbler howled in terror and made frantic efforts to dislodge the bird. Maggie, however, had now recovered his poise and, clinging tenaciously to the lad's coat with his claws, viciously pecked Nibbler on the back of the head.

Snatching up his cap, Happy began to hit Maggie and

succeeded in forcing him from the luckless Nibbler, whose howls and yells were ringing through the trees and scrub. Maggie fell to the grass, but in an instant was air-borne again and flapping rapidly up into his own tree, coming to rest within a few feet of the nest.

Hardly had he settled than a stone, propelled with all the force of which Jacky's catapult was capable, sang past his head. He gave a startled hop and sidled along the branch a little, away from the nest.

"Let him have it as fast as we can, Happy!" shouted Jacky, and Happy responded instantly.

While the two boys kept up a brisk fire, Nibbler dissociated himself from the proceedings. With a choking sob, he intimated that he had had enough and was going home.

As he rushed howling across the paddock, Maggie decided to give him a fitting send-off. Launching himself from the limb, and disregarding the flying stones, he took after the fleeing Nibbler like a pied arrow. Nibbler gave another awful howl as the bird's wings ruffled his hair and then he dived into the security of the scrub where Maggie couldn't get at him.

"Keep an eye on that magpie while I have a go at the nest," said Jacky to Harry. "It won't be safe climbing the tree, but I might be able to bring down a young one if I can blow the nest apart. You stand with your back to mine so that we can see in both directions."

Happy did as he was told and kept his eyes glued on the spot where he had last seen Maggie. That bird had cleared the top of the scrub and was awaiting the appearance of Nibbler on the other side. Perched in a low tree, he was determined to wait there all night if necessary. Nibbler, crouched under a bush, realised this, and was equally determined not to emerge into the open until darkness fell or somebody came and hunted the bird away.

Jacky was quite satisfied with the turn of events. If he could not kill Maggie, he would be satisfied with hunting the bird away from the district. He considered that if he destroyed the nest and the young ones it would have this result. The nest was about fifty feet from the ground and partly obscured by leaves and twigs. Jacky, however, was an expert shot, and a triumphant cry told Happy that he had scored a hit.

Not wanting to be left out of the fun, Happy gave up watching for Maggie's return and joined Jacky in his attack on the nest. Blasted by a continuous barrage of stones, the nest began to show signs of wear and tear, and eventually disintegrated, sticks and twigs flying in all directions.

"Look out! Here they come!" sang out Jacky triumphantly, and Happy joined in the roar of delight as two young fledglings, flapping feeble wings and making frantic efforts to save themselves, dropped through the bottom of the broken nest and, after bumping on limbs and branches, fell heavily to the ground.

"What do you intend to do with them now that you have them?" asked Happy as he and Jacky inspected the young birds lying at their feet.

"They look a bit too young to take home as pets. They've got hardly any feathers on them," said Jacky.

"Leave them where they are."

"Well, now, I don't know," muttered Happy, feeling a

little ashamed now that the excitement was over. "It would be a bit cruel to do that, wouldn't it?"

"Well we can't climb the tree and put them back again because there isn't much of the nest left," said Jacky. "What does it matter, anyway? Who cares about a couple of young magpies? The old birds will look after them."

"I can't see how they can," said Happy, who was now wishing that he had had no hand in the sorry affair.

As it happened, neither of them needed to concern himself about the future welfare of the pitiful little birds. That locality would be the poorer for the loss of two songsters. Both fledglings were dead.

Happy Butt threw a wistful glance over his shoulder as he followed the callous young Peters from the scene of the slaughter. They plunged into the thickets, almost stumbling over Nibbler crouched under his protecting bush. He got up and joined the procession and when the trio emerged on the other side, the watchful Maggie gave a loud squawk of fierce defiance.

Fitting a stone in his catapult, Jacky let fly. The stone hit the branch within an inch of Maggie, startling him a great deal.

He rose into the air and described a circle over their heads, half-minded to attack them. He could see, though, that each of the three had a catapult ready. The odds were too great. So, with a final squawk of defiance, he flew back to the tree that had once contained his nest and family.

Chapter VII.

MAGGIE IS DEFENDED

THE SCHOOL Parents and Citizens' Association meeting had not been very exciting. Members had discussed the usual subjects—the fourth classroom roof needed repairing, there were holes in the playground that should be filled in before some child met with a serious accident, and the headmistress made her usual appeal for more books for the school library. Somebody suggested that a doll and pet show be held to raise funds, another thought a children's frolic would be better, and a third extolled the money-raising virtues of a baby show.

Everything went off comfortably. It was decided to refer several matters to the Minister for Education through the local member of Parliament, and sub-committees were appointed to investigate the possibilities of holding functions to raise money.

"Before the meeting closes, has any member any matter he or she would like to bring forward?" asked the president, hoping that nobody replied, because it was late and he wanted to go home.

Great was his disappointment when Mr. Peters sprang to his feet.

"Yes, I have, a very serious matter," he said. "I want some action taken regarding the vicious magpies that are infesting our parks and attacking people. These birds should all be destroyed. It is becoming a positive danger walking about where there are any trees these days. Many school children have been attacked and it is up to us to protect our children. That is what this association is for."

"Magpies are very useful birds, I believe. They eat insects and things," commented the president, absently.

"They do more than that, Mr. President," said a young lady seated at the back of the hall. "They destroy pests of all kinds and are protected by the Government."

The president was an old gentleman and he vaguely resented this young school teacher saying anything. Little Miss Valentine often said things which he did not like at association meetings. She had too much energy and made him feel tired. The old president was a person who liked to take things easy. He never went looking for trouble and he resented trouble being thrust upon him. Young Miss Valentine often made complaints about things at the school and though he had to admit that she had never yet spoken without justification, still, she was only a bit of a child and, in his opinion, children should be seen and not heard.

"You were saying something about vicious magpies, Mr. Peters?" he asked, ignoring the school teacher.

"Yes, Mr. President, and I have a serious complaint to make about our sergeant of police. Some days ago a magpie savagely attacked my boy Jacky. It pecked him so severely on the head that he was rendered unconscious. Yet, when I complained to the sergeant and asked that the bird be destroyed, do you know what he did?"

"No," replied the president, stealing a look at the clock, "what did he do?"

"Laughed at me," said Mr. Peters angrily. "Laughed at me and said that Jacky was telling lies."

"Did he indeed?" asked the old president, trying to look shocked.

"Yes he did, notwithstanding the fact that Jacky had a big wound in the back of his head," exclaimed Mr. Peters. "As I said before, what use are these birds? It isn't safe to go for a quite walk in any of our parks or gardens. The things swoop down out of trees and bite holes in you.

"What I want this association to do is to launch a drive against magpies in this district and kill them all off," he added savagely.

"Can I ask the speaker a question?" called out a member.

"Er, yes, if you want to," said the president.

"Mr. Peters," said the member — it was young Harry Perkins—"You say that many school children and others have been attacked by dozen of magpies lately. Can you give us the names of these people?"

"No I can't," said Mr. Peters. "I have more to do than take a census of the dozens of people who have been attacked."

"In what park or public garden was your son Jacky attacked?"

"Er, it was not in a public park but in a paddock on the edge of the town," said Mr. Peters, glaring at Perkins. "Anyway, what does that matter?"

"Nothing, except that you have drawn a picture of thousands of magpies infesting our parks. It boils down to one attack in a back paddock," said Perkins.

"There was more than one attack!" exclaimed Mr. Peters.

"So you say, but you can produce no proof," retorted the young farmer. "As to having a killing drive against magpies, you can count me out. It is easy to see that you are not a farmer or you wouldn't talk so foolishly."

"What do you know about it?" demanded Mr. Peters.

"A great deal more than you, obviously," retorted Perkins.

"Now, now, gentlemen, don't let us have any quarrels," interposed the old president. "We are not in Parliament," he added with an attempt at humor.

Mr. Peters, however, was in no mood for airy persiflage.

"It is no use our asking the police for assistance," he said. "Sergeant Grant just laughs at the idea of magpies being vicious. He told me he would do nothing about the bird that pecked my boy. As it so happens, that doesn't matter now, because my Jacky got his revenge on the bird himself."

"Indeed, and did he now! How?" inquired the president.

"He and two of his young friends went down to the paddock with their catapults and blew the nest out of the tree. There were two young ones in it and they killed them. The old birds, I understand, have left the spot."

"Mr. President, ladies and gentleman," he continued, looking around the room, "these three young boys have given us the lead. Are we going to have it said that we elder people allowed the children to do our work for us? What they have started, let us finish. I am going to move a motion that the gentlemen members of this association make a comprehensive drive on magpies in our area and either kill them all or drive them away!"

"Mr. President!" exclaimed Perkins, leaping to his feet.

"Do you second the motion?"

"I certainly do not!" cried the young farmer. "What I want to know is if you intend to accept a motion like that? I say that you cannot. Doesn't Mr. Peters realise that, apart from the absolute barbarism of his motion, he is asking us all to break the law?"

"I must have a seconder for the motion," said the president.

"If you allow such a motion to be discussed by this association," exclaimed the angry young farmer, "you are as bad as this fellow Peters!"

"What do you mean by that remark?" shouted Mr. Peters.

"What I say!"

"How dare you, sir!" exclaimed the President, his dignity outraged. "Resume your seat or leave this meeting. No member shall insult the president while I have the honor to hold that office!"

"I'll second the motion," called out a voice down the back of the hall, and young Perkins sat down fuming.

"Thank you, thank you," said the president, beaming upon the speaker "I shall now ask the meeting to vote."

"Just a moment, Mr. President," cried out Miss Valentine, jumping to her feet with flashing eyes and small fists clenched. "I want to have something to say on this matter. I have never, in all my experience as a teacher of young children, heard anything like the statements made here tonight by Mr. Peters.

"He, a grown man, has glorified a piece of wanton destruction and cruelty by three young larrikins with catapults. He says that Sergeant Grant laughed at him when he told that officer about a magpie attacking his son! Had he told the sergeant what his son and the other two boys did, I think he would have found the sergeant in a different mood.

"I don't know which is the more revolting," she went on passionately, "a man gloating callously over the killing of two young nestlings and wanting respectable, law-abiding people to assist him in killing more, or the three detestable young hooligans who actually did the deed."

"Don't you call my boy a detestable young hooligan," roared Mr. Peters. "I won't have it! I'll report you to your headmistress."

"Don't raise your voice at me, Mr. Peters," she replied icily. "My headmistress is present at this meeting and will scarcely need a report from you. As for calling your boy a hooligan, I repeat it and add that any boy who deliberately murders defenceless birds is a hooligan.

"I want to say this to Mr. Peters, and to any other parent who might harbor similar unworthy thoughts," said the young teacher, "quite apart from the misery endured by the unfortunate birds in their nesting season, it is very, very bad for adults like Mr. Peters to encourage boys to commit callous actions.

"Boys who delight in cruelty grow up to be gangsters, thugs, and criminals, because indifference to the rights and sufferings of other living creatures is the basis of criminal behaviour. The boy who rejoices in smashing the nest containing young birds today will bash old men and children tomorrow."

"Here, here!" said young Perkins, turning admiring eyes upon the indignant Miss Valentine.

"Robbing birds' nests is no less a crime than stealing from a human home," she said. "Parents and teachers should condemn this wanton savagery and strive to educate the children to be kindly and humane. They should not listen for one moment to such suggestions as Mr. Peters has just made. Surely there are among us enough decent people to put a stop to this brutality by guarding these birds, not destroying them, and making all children who own catapults throw them away?

"I just cannot understand Mr. Peters," she continued. "He hears a story from his own son about a magpie rendering him unconscious. Such a thing is almost impossible of belief! Yet, this father, on the mere word of an irresponsible boy, and without attempting, apparently, to prove its truth, would kill hundreds of birds which, incidentally, are protected by the Government! I oppose the motion bitterly."

As Miss Valentine sat down, there was a ripple of applause and before it died away, Perkins was on his feet again.

"I agree with every word the young lady has said," he began. "I want to add a little more to it. Any farmer will tell you of the enormous good that magpies do in destroying agricultural pests. I won't weary you with that. To be fair, though, there have been cases where the birds have become a public nuisance in the nesting season. In such instances they should be destroyed by the proper authorities, not people like Mr. Peters who would kill them all."

"I asked the sergeant to kill one and he wouldn't," put in Mr. Peters.

"And who could blame him on the flimsy evidence you supplied?" retorted Perkins. "One or two birds might become a menace to children and if they do, they should be shot, but why kill many for the sins of one?"

"Do you mean that the birds should be judged on their performances before being shot?" asked a member.

"Yes, but it is a good thing that human beings are not judged on their performances," replied Perkins, glancing at Mr. Peters.

Mr. Peters caught the glance and was indignant.

"Are you suggesting that I should be shot?" he demanded.

"Not necessarily," said the young farmer airily.

"Why, I'll punch you on the nose!" roared Mr. Peters.

"Ladies and gentlemen," said the old president, getting very restless, "please don't let us indulge in recriminations. Really, this discussion is getting us nowhere. Let us finish it off. Does anybody favour Mr. Peters's motion?"

"Yes I do," said Mr. Young, the man who had seconded the motion. "We have heard a lot of sentimental rubbish from Miss Valentine and Mr. Perkins, and I suggest that Miss Valentine keep her lectures on bird lovers for her pupils. As for Mr. Perkins, what he says about magpies doing good for the farmers might be true, but what about the people who are not farmers? What good do magpies do for them?"

"If there were no farmers you would starve," interjected Perkins.

"Never mind that," said Mr. Young irritably. "I agree with Mr. Peters about the need to destroy these vicious birds. They are a deadly danger. What about the boy who was killed by one some years ago? The thing pecked him and its dirty beak caused tetanus. He was taken to hospital and the doctors fought hard to save his life. The hospital did not have enough anti-tetanus serum to check complications, which set in, and they had to send frantic messages all over the State. Special aeroplanes had to be chartered to take the serum hundreds of miles to the hospital but the poor boy's life was not saved.

"Look at the trouble that bird caused. Think of the sorrow of the lad's parents, think of the great expense involved in trying to save his life; yet there are foolish, misguided people like Miss Valentine and Mr. Perkins who would protect these magpies," Mr. Young said heatedly.

"One case against one bird," said Miss Valentine. "Can you name any people in this town who have been attacked by magpies this season?"

"No," admitted Mr. Young "but I believe in getting in first before they have a chance to do any damage."

"We must be fair in this matter," said another member. "While the magpie's usefulness cannot be questioned, he has fallen from grace in some of the States. From 1912 until 1936 a magpie formed the shield of arms of South Australia, but in the latter year they altered it to the sun and three wheat sheafs."

"I don't think that is being fair to the magpie," protested Miss Valentine. "I doubt if it really was a magpie on the South Australian shield. If so, I have never seen such an ingenious bird. According to the design of the shield, the bird shown could perch and fly at the same time. It was not altered because the magpie was in disgrace. As to that, the Australian magpie is not a true magpie. It is a shrike. It's correct name is the piping crow-shrike."

"Order, order!" exclaimed the president. "For goodness sake, ladies and gentlemen, do not let us have a lecture on the habits, names and appearance of this wretched bird. It is getting late. Let us proceed with the motion. The question is, do we kill them, or not?"

"As I was saying," the member went on, "the magpie has fallen from grace a little, mainly because at nesting time he boldly attacks trespassers on what he regards as his domain. He probably has cause to do this, for scores of young magpies have been stolen from nests, the victims of misguided affection of bird lovers who want them as pets. It has often transpired after such attacks that the aid of the police has been secured and the magpie shot."

"Yes, and with its death, and perhaps the deaths of nestlings too young to feed themselves, those localities have become so much the poorer," said Miss Valentine. "So much lost song and lost labor just because a parent bird committed the awful crime of protecting its nest and young."

"What I was leading up to," continued the member patiently, as the young school teacher sat down, slightly embarrassed by her own enthusiasm, "is this: If any person has proper cause to believe that any magpie is dangerous, he should tell the police and ask that it be destroyed. But let him have proper proof and not a wild tale like this of our friend Mr. Peters."

"It is not a wild tale!" exclaimed that gentleman.

"Well, your allegation that our parks and gardens are alive with magpies attacking hundreds of school children, is a wild tale," said the member. "I've heard nothing about it and I get around a lot."

"I believe that in Canberra, the Department of the Interior destroys about 25 a year," put in a member. "They study the birds' performances and an inspector destroys particularly vicious magpies actually detected in attacks."

"Yes, they do not listen to wild tales there," said Miss Valentine meaningly. "Mr. Young has ridiculed me because I am a bird lover. It may interest him to know that it is a common occurrence in London for a policeman to hold up traffic while a duck crosses a street with her young ones, and in Salt Lake City in America, the farmers in the early days erected a monument to gulls who destroyed a locust plague that threatened to ravage their crops."

"One thing everyone seems to have forgotten is that magpies are only vicious during nesting time," said Perkins. "For the rest of the year they are busy keeping down insect pests."

As nobody else had anything to say on the matter, Mr. Peter's preposterous motion was solemnly put to the vote, and was overwhelmingly defeated, only Mr. Peters, Mr. Young and one other member supporting it.

Mr. Peters was very angry about it, and told himself that he would wage a one-man war against the birds, commencing with the one who had started the trouble—Maggie.

But in that he was doomed to be disappointed, because Maggie and his mate, their nest and young ones destroyed, had already left the locality.

Chapter VIII.

TROUBLE ON THE GOLF COURSE

THE SECRETARY of the golf club was angry and he considered that he had every right to be. He went looking for the greenkeeper and found him in his little shed at the rear of the clubhouse.

"O'Brien," he said, without any preliminary greeting, "a magpie is building a nest in that gum tree near the second hole and has been attacking every player on the course. I want you to get down there with your rifle and destroy the thing at once."

"At the second hole, Mr. Murphy?" inquired the greenkeeper. "I didn't know that. I didn't see any magpie when I was down there mowing the green yesterday morning. The bird must have just arrived."

"I know nothing about that," replied the secretary. "All I can say is that there are two birds there now and they have a nest partly built. What is more, the male bird attacked me not ten minutes ago and other players have complained to me that they have been attacked. The thing has got to be destroyed."

"Well, now, Mr. Murphy, I don't like killing magpies," said O'Brien slowly. "They do a lot of good around the course eating crickets and worms that spoil the level surface of the greens. There have been nests on the links before and though one or two caddies have been attacked, I've never known players to suffer."

"Neither have I, O'Brien, but you are missing the point," said the secretary. There is a magpie there now and he is attacking adults. All you have got to do is to go and shoot him, do you hear?"

"I don't like it at all," said O'Brien, shaking his head. "but if you say so, I suppose I must. What I cannot understand is a pair of magpies building a nest now. It is rather late in the season."

"O'Brien," said Mr. Murphy impatiently, "what I require from you is action with your rifle, not with your tongue."

"Very good, sir," said the greenkeeper. "I'll be down there as soon as I can. I can't go straight away as there are several things to attend to here."

"Now you see that that bird is destroyed," said the secretary grimly. "If I find it still there before I go home this afternoon, you will have some pertinent questions to answer."

"I'll do it Mr. Murphy, but I must say I don't fancy it," said O'Brien.

"Never mind what you fancy," retorted the secretary and left O'Brien brooding. He joined his partner and their two caddies and proceeded to the first tee to continue their game. Incidentally, these caddies were none other than Jacky Peters and Nibbler Neville.

Down near the second hole in his gum tree, Maggie was having a quiet time. So vicious had been his attacks that some timid golfers were giving the second hole a wide berth, cutting across country from the first green to the third tee so as to avoid attacks.

As the greenkeeper O'Brien had conjectured, Maggie and his mate had arrived at the tree during the previous afternoon. After the destruction of their nest and family by Jackie Peters, Happy Butt and Nibbler Neville, they decided to leave that locality for good. The golf links were about three miles from the tree that had contained their wrecked home and when they alighted in the old gum near the second green to think things over, its ideal location for a nest struck them simultaneously. Though the season was well advanced, there was still time for them to build another nest and rear a new brood if they set to work at once. They did so, and by the following afternoon when the golf players were beginning to arrive in force on the links, the nest was well under way.

Maggie's treatment at the hands of the three boys had filled him with an intense hatred of the human race, large and small. From now on, the bird told himself, it would be red war. Just let any of them come within range of the new nest and they would suffer for it.

And Maggie had plenty of human subjects upon whom he could vent his dislike. He left the nest building wholly to his mate while he perched in the tree, his feathers quivering with rage as he watched the approach of the first batch of golfers. As each pair neared the green, he launched himself at them, always selecting the nearest. The first intimation the players had of his avenging presence was a quick-snapping beak and a flurry of feathers. Some of them were pecked and others were buffeted by his powerful wings.

Until the arrival of Mr. Murphy, the secretary, and his partner, Maggie had beaten up half a dozen players. Waving clubs, arms and fists and blood-curdling shouts and threats he treated with contempt. He was wise in the ways of these two-legged creatures and was far too agile on the wing to get in the way of a wildly-waved golf club. Shouts and threats left him completely unawed.

As one player remarked to another as they hastened away from the green after the fluttering black and white fury had returned to his tree, the magpie seemed to have gone completely mad. Not once did he attack some parties, but two or three times. The first attack generally caught them all unprepared and as Maggie whirled aloft for another dive, not all of them could hope to escape the second downward plunge. It was most distressing for them.

And so, to avoid these unprovoked attacks a few golfers gave the danger area a miss on their second circuit of the nine-hole course.

But not Mr. Murphy. After he and his partner finished play on the first green and were walking down to the second tee that partner remarked, "We're getting near that magpie's nest again, Joe. Don't you think it would be wise to miss this hole as others have done and thus avoid another attack?"

"No, I don't," said Murphy. "We are playing a competition and if we miss a hole the game falls through. Those who have failed to play the second hole will be disqualified and will have no chance to win the cup. I have narrowly missed winning it for two years now and my heart is set on it this year. Magpie or no magpie, I'm going to play out every hole."

"All right," said his partner, Mr. Angus. "We'll send the caddies on ahead to chase the birds away, eh?"

"No, we'll need them down this fairway," said Murphy, who was playing a good game. His partner's mind, however, was not on his. He was thinking of that magpie down near the second green.

Bisecting the fairway was a creek, a deep creek, and Angus's ball landed some yards from the bank. He swung at it and caused a cloud of dust to rise. When the dust cleared away, the ball was still there, lying on the rim of a gaping hole in the ground.

"Missed it," remarked Nibbler, who was caddying for Murphy. Nibbler was a tactless young rascal.

Angus said nothing, but tried to concentrate on has game. His plan was to hit the ball across the creek and then walk across a small bridge after it. Angus hit the ball into the creek instead.

The silence as they all proceeded to the bank of the creek was nerve-wracking.

"It's in there," remarked Nibbler, pointing unnecessarily at the muddy water.

"Thank you," replied Angus courteously. "I thought it was in Mr. Murphy's hip pocket."

"No. It's in that there dashed creek," said Nibbler.

"I know that!" exclaimed Angus, holding himself in check and refraining from slaying Nibbler with a golf club.

"It's lost," said Jacky Peters, who was caddying for Angus. Deep creek that. Man got drowned in there one day, also a cattle dog."

"Indeed? You interest me," said Angus grimly.

"Well, there will be a caddie added to the list of victims if you don't hurry up and get my ball for me. Jump in and find it, you lazy young devil."

"What?" exclaimed Jacky, looking at Angus in amazement. "Listen, mister, if you think I'm going to hop into that there dashed creek for any dashed golf ball, you must be crazy."

"Here, here, my lad," said Murphy sternly, "that is no way to speak to a member of this club. As to the ball it is undoubtedly lost. Don't worry about it. I have plenty more up at the clubhouse which you can buy."

Mr. Angus spoke to Mr. Murphy and he spoke feelingly. He told the club secretary that he did not like him and he did not like his caddy either. Nibbler looked hurt and wondered why, but Mr. Angus did not enlighten him. Instead, he turned to Jacky and said tersely, "Now, get into that creek and get that ball out and never mind the cheek."

Jacky cautiously approached the creek bank and gazed down into the muddy depths. He then laid aside the golf bag he was carrying and slid down the bank, to stand on the edge of the water. Stare as hard as he could, he was unable to see any sign of the missing ball.

Now, all the antics of these humans had been closely watched by Maggie. The second green was about 100 yards from the creek and the gum tree in which he was perched about 20 yards from the green itself. Angus, Murphy, Jacky and Nibbler were the first people to approach so near for some time. Maggie had been waiting for them to reach the green before he launched his attack, but they had spent so much time at the creek that he began to get restless. Perhaps they would not come any closer, he told himself. Very well, then.

None of the four had any idea of the magpie's scrutiny. They had all completely forgotten him in the discussion about the lost golf ball. Murphy and Angus were standing with Nibbler on the bank while Jacky was leaning over the water and prodding the depths with a golf club.

Then, just as Maggie prepared to strike at Murphy who was the nearest to him, Jacky straightened himself up. The movement caused Maggie to glance at the boy and he recognised him immediately. That boy was one of the young villains who had fired stones at, and wrecked his nest!

Like a dart from a blow-pipe Maggie struck. There was a loud squawk and a terrific howl as Jacky, clapping a hand to a pecked ear, lost his balance and tumbled sideways into the creek, to vanish beneath the dirty water. Startled by the loud splash, the magpie shot into the air and, changing its mind about taking a piece out of Mr. Angus's neck, flew rapidly back to its tree.

"Jacky has fell in the creek," commented Nibbler, gazing with interest at the wavelets caused by his friend's precipitation in the depths.

"Unquestionably, he has," said Murphy and at that moment Jacky's mud-stained face and head shot up into view. He spat out a mouthful of dirty water and then yelled out that he was being drowned.

"You can swim," Nibbler informed him, but made no attempt to help him out. Angus and Murphy lay prone on the ground and each extended a hand to Jacky who grabbed and hung on. They hauled him bodily from the creek and deposited him on the bank. He was quite unharmed, but definitely wet.

"Better go home and get changed," Angus told him. "I'll carry my own bag for the rest of the round."

"That magpie has some use after all," he said to Murphy as Jacky squelched away. "I'm afraid that I couldn't have put up with that boy's impudence much longer."

With a new ball, he played across the creek and both men reached the green without any interference from Maggie. That bird sat up on a high limb and eyed them with intense dislike, but did nothing. He was still a little bewildered by the happening at the creek, but more than content with the trouble he had brought upon Jacky Peters.

When they finished their round and returned to the clubhouse, scores were checked over and it was discovered that Murphy and Angus were all square, or equal, and that their scores were the best. It was resolved that they should play another hole to decide who should be the winner of the cup. So off they went again, and when they had finished the hole, they were still equal.

"We will have to play yet another hole and that means we will have to face that awful magpie again," said Murphy. "Well, there is nothing else to be done, I suppose. Anyway, as soon as we do finish, I shall see to it personally that O'Brien shoots the bird."

"What, after it did me such a good turn in disciplining that cheeky caddy?" said Angus with a laugh. Murphy, however, did not think it was funny, and said so. Golfers, he added, must be protected.

Maggie was not in his tree when Angus and Murphy

approached the creek again. He had seen movements down on the green and was busily inspecting the ground, hopping and running around the smooth grass and looking for stray crickets and worms.

"Knock that magpie flying," said Murphy viciously to Angus as Angus prepared to play his ball.

"But it isn't flying. It's on the ground," said Angus with a grin.

"Oh, yes, be funny, be funny!" snarled Murphy. He was not in the best of tempers, because his game had been so bad at this last hole that his chances of winning had practically disappeared. When they had crossed the creek, Murphy was behind Angus in the scoring and it meant that the next ball he hit would have to go into the hole on the green for him to have a chance. The hole was fifty yards away and only a miracle or a fluke would send the ball straight into it.

Angus swung his club and sent the ball straight and true. It landed within a few feet of Maggie and ran up under his very beak. Maggie was standing several yards from the hole and got the surprise of his life. What was this thing? It looked like an egg. He pecked it and found it to be very hard. It did not look worth eating.

Though he had been on the links for a couple of days, he had not before seen a golf ball at close quarters. Most of his time had been spent in swooping at the heads of players and caddies and then returning to his tree for another attack.

"Leave that ball alone, you villain!" howled Angus, waving his club wildly. Maggie took no notice. He was too absorbed in the ball. He cocked his head on one side and studied it carefully and then made another peck at it.

"I hope he doesn't pick it up and fly off with it," said Angus.

"It doesn't matter, I mean, apart from the cost of the ball," said Murphy. "You can place another one at the same spot without being penalised. You ought to hit it into the hole with one stroke, or two at the outside. If you take two, your score will be six. My next shot will be my fifth and unless I put it into the hole from here, I've got no chance in life of beating you."

He broke off suddenly.

"Leave that ball alone, you black and white thief!" he yelled at Maggie, who was pecking away at it. Angus and Murphy feared that the bird would seize it in his beak at any moment and depart with it.

It was a really fascinating object, Maggie considered. He pecked it and it rolled a few inches. He hopped after it and gave it another nudge.

"If I can't win the cup, I can try to save O'Brien a job by killing that wretched magpie," said Murphy savagely. "Watch me knock it into the middle of next week."

He swung his club and sent the ball high in the air straight for the green. By this time Maggie was only a foot from the hole. The ball landed with a plop a yard away from him, bounced and hit him fair on the wing. Thus deflected from a course which would have taken it past the hole, it bounced again, lobbed on the green and fell into the hole, dropping cleanly past the flag stick.

Maggie gave one indignant squawk of surprise ere he made for his tree at full speed.

"Did you see that?" breathed Murphy.

"I saw it!" exclaimed Angus. "It looks to me as if your friend Maggie has won the cup for you."

"Are you trying to be funny?" growled the club secretary.

"I am not," said his friend. "You can't be disqualified for that, you know. It would have been a far different matter if Maggie had pushed the ball into the hole. Then you would have had to replace it as I have to do now that the bird shoved mine about four feet from where it was."

"Yes, I see what you mean," said Murphy slowly and thoughtfully.

The two men walked to the green. Angus picked up his ball and placed it as near as possible to the spot where it had landed and from where Maggie had pushed it—about ten feet from the hole.

Murphy had taken five shots with the assistance of Maggie. Angus was then four. If he holed his putt, they would again be equal. Carefully he played the shot. The ball trickled to within an inch of the hole and then stopped dead. Angus tapped it into the cup. He had taken six.

"Congratulations, Murphy," he said, holding out his hand.

"Don't congratulate me!" said the secretary. "Give three cheers for my old friend Maggie up in that tree!"

He took off his cap and waved it. Maggie did not understand the gesture, but he objected, on principle, to any human being waving things at him. He felt half-inclined to dive down at this fellow and peck a piece out of his ear.

On the way back to the club house, Murphy and

Angus met O'Brien. The greenkeeper had a rifle and a gloomy look.

"What are you going to do with that gun, O'Brien?" demanded Murphy.

"To shoot that there magpie like you told me to and I don't like it," said the greenkeeper.

"I should think not!" exclaimed the secretary. "Here, give me that gun! Don't you know that magpies are valuable birds and are rightly protected by the law? You can't go around shooting them as you like!"

"But you told me to, sir!" protested the amazed O'Brien.

"I've changed my mind. You leave that bird alone. What is more, put up a notice on the board saying that Maggie is not to be harmed. No, I'll do it myself."

Saying which, Murphy strode away cheerily. The bewildered O'Brien caught Angus by the sleeve.

"Excuse me, Mister Angus," he said, "but is Mister Murphy all right? He hasn't got a touch of the sun or anything, has he?"

Angus laughed and told the interested greenkeeper of the part played by the reprieved magpie in the shot that had won Murphy the cup.

"I think that is one magpie that will be allowed to nest in peace if Mr. Murphy has anything to do with it," he added.

"So they all should be," said O'Brien. "I've got a lot of time for magpies."

Chapter IX.

MAGGIE FINDS A FRIEND

The story of how Maggie won the golf cup for Mr. Murphy, the club secretary, became one of the favorite stories among members. When one humorist bestowed upon him the nickname of "Magpie Murphy," it clung to him, but the secretary did not mind at all.

Had Maggie been endowed with human understanding and learned of the good turn he had done a hatred human being, he would have felt intensely angry. He would have resented, too, the fact that he had been placed under the special patronage and protection of a human being.

Far from desiring to kill Maggie now, the golf club secretary adopted him as a mascot, and a fierce and recalcitrant mascot he was. During the hatching period and when the young birds were in the nest, he protected them with all the energy of which he was capable. Golfers approaching his nest found him about their ears. Some players instructed their caddies to go ahead of them and act as decoys. Their role was to allow Maggie to attack them while the golfers played out the hole in peace.

There was some difficulty about this. In the first place, several of the caddies objected to being made targets for a sharp beak, even though "Magpie Murphy" had announced that he would recompense adequately any boy who was pecked. The lads considered that a shilling or two was poor compensation for a lacerated ear or a wounded skull. Others, however, were willing to take a sporting chance.

Things, however, did not always work out as expected. Sometimes Maggie disregarded the caddies and went for the golfers. There was some talk among these of asking the president to call a special meeting of the club to over-rule the secretary and have Maggie shot out of hand as the world's prize nuisance. Before any definite action could be taken, however, Maggie's offspring were ready to emerge into the world, and with their exit from the nest to hunt for themselves on the ground, Maggie's belligerence eased and finally died away altogether.

The golf course, hitherto, had been worked by several pairs of magpies, but none of these birds had been nesting on the links this season. They had their own special breeding areas in other parts. The nesting season over, however, they returned with their broods to the course and Maggie and his mate and their youngsters joined them.

The golf club property was large enough to support many of the black and white songsters, and they lived together amicably enough, covering the course for food during the day and roosting in convenient trees at night.

Unlike his venerable parent, Old Broken Beak, Maggie was not bad-tempered in between nestings; in fact he was sociably inclined, as was his mate. Their youngsters stayed with them, learning magpie lore, all that season. As for the golfers, the whole flock just ignored them. They often saw these people playing, hitting white balls and walking after them but had no inclination to attack them. One young fledgling did try to eat a ball but found the hard rubber not to his taste, so left it alone.

As summer gave way to winter, the birds conformed to routine. Very sociable, they fed harmoniously together and often descended to playing games, indulging in mimic fights, chasing each other around the place, playing hide and seek in the long grass and generally conducting themselves in gentlemanly and innocent fashion.

With the arrival of August once more, and the need to build again, Maggie and his mate debated whether they should use the same tree on the golf links or seek another. The events of the previous year had been forgotten in the off-season, but with nesting time at hand, memory came back in a flood. It had been a worrying and a strenuous time for Maggie. The golf links were always crowded with interfering human beings, large and small, and the bird had been kept busier attending to them than he had been in any season he could recall.

Maggie and his mate decided to have a look around the district for another suitable tree. If none were to be found, then they would have to use the golf links.

One morning in late winter they went exploring. Avoiding every place in which they had built in other years, the birds combed the district for many miles, and in due course came to Perkins's farm. Maggie recognised it as they were flying over. He dimly recalled following a plough and feasting on fat white grubs, worms and crickets. The very thought of it made his beak water and he planed down to have a closer look. Now, if only there were a handy tree. There was.

It was a large Moreton Bay fig. The only drawback was that it was growing rather close to a house. Maggie did not want to associate again with human beings or live in their houses, but that tree and its close proximity to land that might be ploughed at any time—not forgetting the young wheat in Farmer Higgin's fields hard by—was attractive.

With his mate, he flew down and alighted in the fig. Yes, it was a very suitable nesting place. As for the human occupants of the house, well, he felt quite capable of dealing with them.

It was with surprise and delight that Harry Perkins, a day or so later, observed the two magpies busily constructing their nest in a fork of the tree. Magpies always had been his favorite birds and he intended, if he could, to win the friendship of this pair. He knew it would be a difficult task at nesting time, but he was determined to persevere

During the building operations, Maggie and mate did not trouble about the man, and they picked up the pieces of raw meat he left in handy places without caring whose hand provided them. No ground had been ploughed during this period and they had to search distant paddocks for food—there were none really close to the farm. Maggie and his mate did not mind searching for food; in any event, that was the cardinal law of their lives. The Creator of birds provided food but He did not throw it into their nests.

Perkins, in leaving pieces of raw meat around the place, was laying the ground-work of his campaign to win the birds' friendship. He had it worked out that when the nestlings came and both parents were kept busy finding food for their hungry young mouths, Maggie and Mrs. Maggie would be glad to find food on the ground under the nest, thus saving long flights to distant paddocks. If the birds knew that he provided this food, they might feel kindly disposed towards him. Perkins, of course, did not know that Maggie was daily hoping that he would plough up some ground.

No sooner had the eggs been laid and Mrs. Maggie started brooding, than Maggie took up his inherited role of sentinel; and Perkins, naturally, was his first target. The young farmer, though it cost him mental and physical effort, ignored the bird's first charge. He was walking across his yard when it took place and he kept steadily on his way as the angry bird squawked about his head. Whirling aloft, Maggie dived again, and again the man ignored him. Puzzled, the bird returned to his tree and did not attack again.

Perkins repeated the procedure daily, and eventually it was driven home to Maggie that he had nothing at all to fear from this man. With that realisation, he ceased attacking him. He had one go at old Farmer Higgins on the adjoining property and was rewarded with several hearty curses; but, after that, observing that the old farmer did not come within a quarter of a mile of the nest, decided that there was nothing to fear from him either.

With regard to the pieces of raw meat that Perkins regularly placed on stones in half a dozen places around the yard, Maggie was wiser than Perkins gave him credit for. His memory harked back to his first year of life as a pet in a backyard. He had got raw meat there. He had never found any in his wild state. Intelligent bird that he was, he connected raw meat, which he loved, with human beings, and this made him more tolerant of Perkins. Parental love and the primitive urge to protect his nest and family, were too deep at this time of the year for him to be wholly friendly.

Maggie was quite unafraid of Perkins, and when the young farmer threw pieces of raw meat and sometimes a grub or two on the ground just outside the back door, Maggie flew down from his tree and collected them. At first he would not do this while the man was in sight, but with the coming of his three voraciously-hungry young ones, he could not afford to stand too much on ceremony. He had come to depend upon that raw meat as an essential part of his diet and that of his family.

It soon became mere routine for Perkins to stand at the back door and throw down delicacies, and for Maggie to drop out of the tree and pick them up while the farmer stood a few yards away. Mrs. Maggie was a little hesitant at first, but she, too eventually joined in. Perkins, of course, did not supply them with all the food they needed. They still had to go hunting. But they could always depend upon human-provided food in the early mornings and before sunset.

One day Perkins decided to get on with the ploughing. That was the day for which Maggie had been waiting. When he saw the farmer harness the horses to the plough, he grew excited and fluttered and squawked around a few yards above. Hardly had the plough bitten into the deep, rich, brown earth, than he was into the furrow. Seizing a large white grub, he departed with it swiftly, and when he returned his mate was with him. There were plenty of earth creatures being turned up, and the two birds were as busy as bees gobbling them up, ever and anon flying off to their nest with tasty morsels for the youngsters.

Perkins was delighted with the whole affair and his affection for the two birds grew daily. He hoped that when their family was old enough to leave the nest, the five birds would stay around the farm.

It was a glad day for him when Maggie and mate were accompanied to the furrows by three young ones. He still provided them with meat, but now the nestlings were big enough to fly around and forage for themselves, it eased the work of the parents.

Maggie's antagonism had long since vanished. His attitude now was quite friendly. His mate was more aloof and so were the young birds. Maggie was recalling his year as the pet of the Jones family. Of that brief year he had only pleasant memories.

The magpie family became attached to the farm and Perkins had little cause to complain about their behaviour. To him their early morning choir in the fig tree was the most heavenly music he had ever heard. He regretted that Maggie's mate one day saw fit to kill a small yellow thornbill that flew into the fig tree. He saw the whole unfortunate episode. The small tom-tit, chirping merrily, alighted on a twig just below where the magpie family was sheltering from the hot rays of the sun. Mrs. Maggie immediately dropped down on it and, seizing it in her beak, returned to the limb above. There she quickly consumed the small bird under the lazy eyes of her family.

One morning, Perkins, returning from the back paddock to the homestead to get some article he needed, noticed Maggie and his family behaving peculiarly. The five birds were feeding around a large patch of beans when he first noticed them and he paused idly to watch them.

Suddenly Maggie raised his head and looked at the sky. Then he flew on top of the harness shed, squawking loudly. Immediately his whole family joined him. The five birds sat in a row gazing fixedly towards the west and then, as one, they took off flying rapidly in a line.

The young farmer followed their flight with astonished eyes. What could be the matter with the birds? Then he saw.

Away to the west and advancing rapidly to meet the fleeting magpies, was a dark, undulating cloud which rose and fell, but came rushing onwards.

"Higgins!" bellowed Perkins, wheeling round and rushing madly across the bean patch, trampling down plants as he did so.

"What's the trouble, young fellow?" exclaimed the old farmer, emerging from a barn.

"Plenty!" panted Perkins. "Look at that!"

He pointed a grim finger at the rapidly-approaching cloud.

"Grasshoppers!" he shouted. "Come on, man, we've got to work and work fast!"

Chapter X

THE GRASSHOPPER PLAGUE

Out on the vast plains of the west and north-west, strange events were taking place in the warm spring sunshine. As far as the eye could reach in any direction, miniature holes were appearing in the hard earth—not ones or twos, or tens and hundreds, but thousands upon thousands.

And from these holes there emerged in their battalions, creatures slightly resembling large fleas, which hopped and skipped merrily in the sunshine. Hours before, this vast tract of land had been practically devoid of life, except for a melancholy crow carking dismally, a lizard scampering across the ground, and a rabbit lazing in the shade of a stunted tree. Now it appeared that nature had gone mad. As the hordes of young wingless grasshoppers hatched from their eggs below the surface of the hard earth emergence was, in some mysterious manner, conveyed to birds throughout the length and breadth of the land. Where there had been one crow there were now hundreds. Great flocks of ibises, hawks, wood-swallows, magpies and other birds, assembled for the feast and as the young 'hoppers attacked the grass, so did the birds attack them.

But what impression did it make upon the hopping horde? In countless numbers they vanished as the countless birds fed and fed again, but more and more of them emerged from the egg-beds below.

As the days passed, the grass supply vanished and soon it was necessary for the 'hoppers to migrate to fresh pastures. Migrate the voracious insects did, moving forward in all directions and in a densely-packed mass. Through their ranks fluttered armies of ibises, crows, magpies and other large birds, while smaller ones swooped, pecked, ate, swooped, pecked, ate, until they could eat no more. Magpies and ibises and crows did not trouble to fly. They just walked through the millions and consumed such numbers that at last they could not fly if they wanted to.

Forward, ever forward numbers undiminished swept the 'hopper plague, its ranks continually added to by local swarms. As the young 'hoppers ate, they increased in size, and so fast did they grow that they were continually shedding old skins and appearing in new ones which would allow of further expansion. Their suits never had a chance to get shabby—they were not worn long enough.

Within a few weeks their wings began to appear, and presently the 'hoppers were endowed with the means to cover long distances easily.

Disregarding the presence of their feathered enemies which continued to take great toll, the insects were now ready for the great adventure. Before they grew their wings they had been forced to hop along and eat what grass they happened to find; but the acquisition of wings filled them all with a strange restlessness, an urge to move and keep on moving. Onwards pressed the horde, now many miles in width and depth. Seldom rising high from the ground, they flew on, but not together. Thousands alighted to feed, but were soon on the wing again, while others dived to earth. Thus there was a continuous stream of rising and settling 'hoppers. Where they landed they stripped the earth of every vestige of greenness. The air was filled with them, the sun glittered on their wings and the noise they made was like that of a strong wind.

"I've never seen anything like it for years," said Old Higgins to young Perkins as they stood together looking, with grim eyes, at what was left of their green crops. They had done what they could in the way of poison baits, but what chance had they against those countless millions? Heaps of dead 'hoppers littered the farmlands, but the great swarm had passed on to other places.

What incensed old Higgins was the fact that the hungry hordes had added insult to injury. Not satisfied with eating his crops, they had devoured some washing he had hanging on the line! His second best shirt now reposed in the bodies of numerous grasshoppers!

"Come inside, Perkins, and have a cup of tea," he said at last. "Don't let us stand out here torturing ourselves."

"I could do with a drink of strong tea," said Perkins, following the elder man into the house. Inside was more evidence of the pest. Dozens of the things were crawling around the walls, the floor and the ceiling, and patches of bare boards showed that some of the hungry insects had a pretty taste for wallpaper.

Irritably brushing a number of the things from the table, Higgins set out two big cups and than made the tea. Both he and Perkins were bachelors.

"I'll switch on the radio while you are making the tea,

if you don't mind. A little music might brighten us up," said Perkins.

"All right," said Higgins.

But no cheerful music came from the wireless.

"The grasshopper menace is becoming more serious in four States," came the announcer's voice.

"Switch the thing off," exclaimed Higgins. "Isn't it bad enough seeing the destruction to your own property, without having to listen to it over the air?"

"Just a moment," said Perkins. "Apparently we are not the only sufferers. Let us hear how widespread this plague is."

"Millions of insects have destroyed large areas of wheat in the Darling Downs district of Queensland," came the announcer's voice. The country has been stripped of all green herbage and the swarms are so thick that trains have been held up. Crushed bodies of grasshoppers have made the rails so slippery that the wheels cannot grip and sand has had to be used liberally so that trains may proceed slowly.

"The New South Wales Department of Agriculture has warned farmers and graziers in the north, north-west and west, and irrigation area pastoralists against flying swarms of plague grasshoppers which are on the move. The danger area covers the Riverina, the west and the north-west plains. Mixing stations for poison bran have been set up in various strategic areas. All farmers should be on the watch for the first indication of flying swarms and should have baits ready to bait the swarms as soon as they get into crops."

"A lot of good it did us," said Perkins bitterly.

"Oh, for a flock of ten million magpies," said old Higgins with a grim smile.

"Millions of grasshoppers are still ravaging rich vegetable and wheat areas in the Murray River flats of Victoria," said the radio. Specially-equipped R.A.A.F. planes have poison-sprayed the area, but have failed to stop the grasshoppers. Flame-throwers, poisoned baits and sprays are being used in an effort to stop the swarms."

"It sounds just like a communique during a war, doesn't it?" commented Perkins. "Well, it is a war: the farmer against the greatest pest in modern times."

"And in ancient times, too," said Higgins. "Europe, Asia and America were plagued with locusts long before Australia was heard of."

"In South Australia," droned the radio announcer, "the 'hoppers are on the wing in plague numbers. In towns some householders are having difficulty in opening their doors because the pests are clustered on verandahs to a depth of six inches. The outside wall of some houses are covered. In one case, 'hoppers got inside a house, ate all the wallpaper and nearly filled a bathtub with their bodies. Myriads of the pests in the north-south railway area have forced engine drivers to brush 'hoppers from the rails so that trains may be kept moving.

"Flower gardens have been eaten out and fruit trees, tomato patches and lettuce plantations have been stripped. Motor cars driving through the dense swarms have been forced to stop because their radiators have been chocked with 'hoppers bodies."

"Switch it off, Perkins," begged Higgins. "I've listened to all I can stand."

"So have I," said the younger man.

Together they left the house and once more surveyed their stricken lands.

It was a week later. Perkins had done what he could to repair the damage caused by the invaders, but there was little he could salvage from the ruins.

Even the Moreton Bay fig tree had suffered through the insatiable appetites of the winged curse.

Another blow to Perkins was the fact that Maggie and family apparently had deserted him. Well, he mused over a lonely breakfast, he could not condemn the birds. They were untrammelled creatures, free to come and go as they desired; and he honored them for the way they had flung themselves into the battle against the advancing hordes—pitting their puny strength against an irresistible torrent.

Where were they now, he wondered. Probably following the swarm as it devastated other areas many miles away.

He got up from the table and began to wash up his breakfast things. As he did so, the first rays of the rising sun filtered through the curtained kitchen window.

And as the beams danced on the table, turning the steel knife, fork and spoon into wondrous points of glittering light, the grandeur of the morning was dramatically enhanced by a glorious burst of melody that filled the room as a choir might fill a mighty cathedral. First one voice and then another, the beautiful flute-like melody rose and fell on the placid air.

Young Perkins rushed to the door and flung it open. There, in the now ragged fig tree, were four black and white birds, pouring out their very hearts in indescribable melody.

Maggie and his family had returned.

Listening to the wild beauty of the song, young Harry Perkins began to feel a different man. In those free and unfettered notes he heard hope for the future and a promise of greater things to come. He was young and Australia was a grand country. There was work to be done and there were hands to do it. What if he had received a great set-back? Had not his fathers before him, when they set out to win a new continent from the wilds, encountered many set-backs, infinitely harder than any he had known?

His heart swelling with new resolve, he gave himself up wholly to the delight of listening to the magpie melody. He felt like one inspired.

Maggie and his family became mute. They, too, had work to do. One by one they dropped down to Mother Earth and, with busy beaks, commenced energetically to hunt for their breakfasts.

Perkins looked at them affectionately.

"Thank you, Maggie," he said softly. "A new day has begun for me, too."

THE END